H.E. BATES

Flying bombs over England

EDITED BY BOB OGLEY

Author's royalties will be donated
to the RAF Benevolent Fund

Published by Froglets Publications supported
by Kent County Council Arts and Libraries

Froglets Publications Ltd

Brasted Chart,
Westerham, Kent TN16 1LY.

Tel: 0959 562972
Fax 0959 565365

ISBN 1 872337   18 X (paperback)
ISBN 1 872337 04 X (hardback)

Cover illustrations

Front: Polish fighter ace Tadeusz Szymanski, in a Mustang, gets a good look at a flying bomb on July 12, 1944, over the town of Hastings.
By Graham Coton.

Back: Death of a doodlebug.
By Colin Frooms.

This book was originated by Froglets Publications Ltd, printed and paperbound by Staples Printers Rochester Ltd, Neptune Close, Medway City Estate, Rochester, Kent ME2 4LT. Casebound by Green Street bindery.

Jacket design by Alison Stammers

A special thank you to **Fern Flynn** and **Jill Goldsworthy** who were greatly involved with the production at all stages.

The painting on the cover, which is reproduced by courtesy of the artist, Graham Coton, recreates a unique and courageous feat in the battle in the air against Hitler's flying bombs. The pilot of the Mustang III is Warrant Officer Tadeusz Szymanski (pictured above in later life), a tenacious Polish ace who was on combat mission with 316 Squadron on the afternoon of July 12, 1944 when he spotted a doodlebug on course for London. At the time he was over the sea, off the coast of Dungeness. This is Tadeusz's own story of the events that followed.

"I started shooting and saw strikes before my ammunition was finished, but the bomb kept on a dead-level course. Over the town of Hastings I moved into close formation to get a close look at it. The thing was jerking along and the elevator was flapping with each vibration of the crude jet motor. I noticed there were no ailerons and on the front of the bomb was a silly little propeller. It looked ridiculous. We didn't know at the time but this was the aiming device set to dive the bomb into the ground after so many miles.

"I decided to try and tip the doodlebug up with my wing tip. The flight was controlled by gyroscopes and if you turn a gyroscope more than 90 degrees it goes haywire. As soon as I put my port wing under the doodlebug's wing, it started lifting and I banked to starboard. I repeated this manoeuvre eleven times but each time it went over so far and then came back. By now the barrage balloons protecting London were in sight and I was becoming rather anxious.

"I tried a different manoeuvre, hitting it very hard with my wing tip as I went up into a loop. When I recovered my position I found, to my dismay, that the doodlebug was flying perfectly safe and level — but upside down! Suddenly it dived out of control and crashed in open countryside."

CONTENTS

Diagrams and statistics, which may be helpful in following the story of the V1 and V2 appear on P. 154 and P. 155. There is a special section in colour between P. 148 and P. 160

FOREWORD

A symbol of Kent's ordeal

IN August, 1930 a young H.E.Bates took his bride-to-be, Madge, on a long walk from Canterbury to the village of Pluckley in the Weald of Kent. "As we toiled up the last mile or two", he later wrote, "we passed a small church standing on a grassy hillock above a stream. Sheep were grazing under the old stone walls and Madge paused to take a photograph. We didn't know until later that that church was to become a closer part of our lives."

A year later, the couple, newly-married, returned to Little Chart, near Pluckley to live. They had bought a barn for conversion, one mile from the church, which was unique in that it contained a Roman Catholic chapel under its Protestant roof. In that peaceful Kent village they settled down to live happily together for more than 40 years.

It was not always peaceful. In his autobiography, *The World in Ripeness,* H.E. wrote of "a dark and chilling air of doom" which arrived in "my own piece of pastoral England" in the summer of 1944. "Soon after D Day, I was home on leave for two or three days when I woke in the middle of the night to a great and hideous noise and the sight of what was clearly a burning aircraft flying low over the roof of the house. I had never seen a burning aircraft flying so low at night but within minutes it was followed by another, then another and yet another. All were flying in the same direction, that is north-westwards towards London, at the same height and with the same hideous racket. I was greatly mystified and, with four young children in the house, not a little frightened.

"Morning solved the mystery; these were Hitler's malevolent flying bombs, aptly named doodlebugs, launched in formidable numbers, without respite and with the object of causing infinite disaster to London and infinite damage to the morale of the civilian population."

Later, he wrote: "On a beautiful August evening in 1944, a doodlebug floated over my house, cut out half a mile away and fell with an almighty bang. It had ended its flight on top of the church tower under which, so many years before, Madge and I had paused to watch a flock of sheep safely graze".

The church was St Mary of the Holy Rood at Little Chart. The doodlebug was shot down by a fighter a few minutes after 8 pm on August 16, 1944. It landed on the Norman tower and six bells came crashing down, followed by the walls. Today, almost 50 years after that tragedy, the ivy-covered remains of Little Chart Church remain as a symbol of Kent's ordeal in the summer of 1944. H.E. and Madge Bates were among those who campaigned to keep it this way.

It was less than two weeks after the 1944 incident that H.E. Bates ,

then on holiday in Scotland with Madge, received a telegram ordering him back to London. There he was told to fly to France "the sole object of which was to seek out and report on doodlebug launching sites in the area of Picardy and Pas de Calais."

The church at Little Chart, hit by a doodlebug on August 16, 1944.

INTRODUCTION
Why this story was suppressed

TWO weeks after the first flying bombs crashed on English soil in June 1944, a Wing Commander in PR3 branch of the Air Ministry wrote to the Director of Public Relations suggesting that a small pamphlet should be prepared, describing the V1 campaign and published on completion of the (anticipated) British triumph. The project was approved and entrusted to the Air Ministry's writer in residence, Squadron Leader H.E.Bates.

Recruited a few years earlier to the Public Relations Branch, Bates had already written several stories about the bomber crews under the pseudonym 'Flying Officer X'. These were a great success.

H.E. was delighted to be given the task of writing the 'Flying Bomb' pamphlet and even more delighted to be ordered to fly to France to "seek out the launching sites in the area of Picardy and Pas de Calais". He had been told to take all the time he wanted, go where he wanted and have a look at Paris while he was there. He embarked on his mission, anxious to prove that chief credit for defeating the flying bomb rested with the RAF.

Back home, complications began to emerge. The original plan was for a modest 5,000 word pamphlet, produced by the RAF and similar to the highly successful publication *The Battle of Britain* which had been written earlier in the war by Hilary St George Saunders. The War Office became involved in the new project. So did the Ministry of Home Security, the Ministry of Information and the Ministry of Health. Meetings of all various representatives were held, memos flew back and forth and a press conference was arranged. By September it was decided that the scale of the flying bomb assault on England and the way it was contained, warranted a 40,000-word book.

Scores of civil servants were anxious that their particular ministerial department should share the credit for this ambitious publication. The only interested party missing was the author himself — H.E. was still in France, touring the launching sites, meeting the troops, talking to villagers and learning much more about the brilliantly conceived flying robots and what the British bombers had done to the French countryside.

Returning to his office in PR3, Squadron Leader Bates set to work on the now-enlarged publication. As he typed, the sound of V2 rockets zoomed out of the stratosphere to crash in the distance and flying bomb attacks resumed — many of them air-launched from Heinkel aircraft. He requested more details, particularly of Allied losses, and was told by Air Intelligence "that there were strong security objections against publishing such figures". On March 2, 1945, before the last of Hitler's secret weapons fell on British soil, Bates was informed that his almost-finished manuscript must be treated as secret until passed by the censor.

With this ruling, controversy raged. Wing Commander Dudley Barker who had been fighting for the publication of the book since June, 1944, demanded to know whether Bates' great effort was to be wasted. No clear answer was forthcoming. Meanwhile, the War Cabinet joined the argument by instructing the Ministry of Information to issue a book about all the Crossbow* operations. Wing Cmdr Barker asked for further guidance. Was Bates' work to be used as a basis for this? Still there was no ruling.

On May 11, 1945 — three days after VE Day — Barker wrote: "I gather, confidentially, that the truth is the Ministry of Information are extremely loath to produce any book at all if they are not to be allowed to explain the Mimoyecques installation as they feel that, now the German war is over, to withhold information would be to deceive the public." He was right. Months later an internal Air Ministry memo explained that "unless a chapter on these structures is included, the pamphlet will lose much of its appeal to the public".

The fact is that the public knew nothing about the existence of the Mimoyecques installations and were to know nothing until other writers, years later, described the existence of a gigantic long-range gun capable of firing rocket shells at London. This was the V3. It contained 50 smooth-bore barrels, 416 feet long which would have fired finned projectiles, each weighing 300 lbs at a combined rate of up to 10 a minute at London. The battery was found by advancing forces at Mimoyecques, near Calais. Fortunately it had been heavily bombed and could never have been used.

There was one final attempt to save the manuscript. On November 1, 1945, Mr Cecil Day-Lewis of the Publications Division of the Ministry of Information suggested that details of Mimoyecques could

*Crossbow was the name of the War Cabinet Committee charged with finding out more about the existence of Hitler's secret weapons.

6

H.E.Bates' early career as a well-received but penniless young writer was transformed by the wartime commission from the Air Ministry which took him as a roving correspondent, not only to France, but also to India and Burma. His Flying Officer X stories captured the tense atmosphere of the times as he portrayed the brief lives of the bomber pilots. This paved the way for real success. His many other celebrated books include The Poacher, Fair Stood the Wind for France, The Jacaranda Tree, Love for Lydia and the Darling Buds of May in which he created the much-loved Larkin family. H.E.Bates CBE, died in 1974 aged 69.

be described. "All the Chiefs of Staff ask", he wrote, "is for a formal security review of the actual text." Day-Lewis, a friend of H.E Bates and, destined to become Poet Laureate, also failed to save his fellow writer's work.

Time finally ran out. H.E. Bates was demobbed along with many of his colleagues in PR3 and the attempt to publish his story of the flying bombs was abandoned. By deciding it should be suppressed for 30 years, the Air Ministry denied the public access to a superbly written story about a crucial period of air warfare.

The manuscript lay in the Public Record Office for several more years until it was seen by Bob Ogley, while researching his book *Doodlebugs and Rockets*. He sought permission from H.E.Bates' widow, Madge, to publish it in time for the 50th anniversary of the doodlebug campaign. She requested that the royalties from the sale of the book be directed to the RAF Benevolent Fund.

Here it is — a brilliant and vivid portrait of 30,000 words about the flying bombs and rockets, their concept, development and the totally indiscriminate nature of their subsequent use. Readers must bear in mind that the story was actually composed before the war ended and long before the full, tragic details of both military and civilian losses had become known. The manuscript has not been altered in any way; the words are those of H.E.Bates, circa 1945 and some descriptions may seem, by today's standards, rather outdated.

However, in order to give the reader a fuller picture of the Vengeance Campaign which history has revealed, Bob Ogley has added contemporary photographs with captions giving greater detail. Also included are many photographs of sites in France and England as they exist today.

H.E., in 1944, also wrote the enormously successful *Fair Stood the Wind For France,* but here his descriptions of rural France had been written entirely from imagination. In his autobiography he wrote about his trip to France later in 1944. "It was one of much reward and excitement but my visit proved, not for the first or last time, that imagination can take a writer nearer to the heart of the truth than any amount of observation and that instinct, rather than sheer reasoning, will guide him just as surely."

Extracts from the letters

JUNE 26, 1944

The original idea for a "pamphlet" on the flying bombs came from Wing Commander Dudley Barker of PR3. On June 26, 1944, less than two weeks after the first V1 crashed on British soil, he wrote to the Air Ministry.

"Would you please care to consider a suggestion that we should prepare immediately a small pamphlet on "The Battle of the Flying Bomb". My feeling is that within a reasonably short time the flying bomb operations will be finished for good......

"The whole story, therefore, of the RAF's measures to combat the menace will by that time be a neat, compact and quite distinctive episode of the war....

"There has been a tendency to criticise the RAF (unjustifiably of course) because the people of southern England have been subjected to this bombardment, which still continues. I suggest that it would do a great deal to quell this criticism and to re-establish whatever prestige may have been lost, if a pamphlet were ready for publication very soon after the attacks finished."

SEPT 11, 1944

A meeting was held at the Air Ministry to discuss the "pamphlet". Present was Mr George Griffiths, public relations officer of the Ministry of Home Security who said:

"The pamphlet should give a clear and overall picture of the whole battle including the work of the Civil Defence Services and descriptions of the way the general public faced the attack. It would also be necessary to give a good account of the organisation behind the flying bomb attack and the tracks the bombs pursued".

Mr Griffiths was told Squadron Leader Bates had already been sent to inspect the launching sites in France and, if possible, to interview members of the German launching crews.

MAY 11, 1945

Mr Robert Fraser, deputy controller of production for the Ministry of Information wrote to PR3 to tell them that the War Cabinet wanted a book to be prepared dealing with the Crossbow weapons as a whole.

"You already have a copy of the first draft text which Bates prepared which deals exhaustively with the V1 and scantily with the V2. This is being prepared under the censorship of the War Office, the Ministry of Home Security, the Ministry of Health and the Air Ministry. It is my intention now to ask Bates to include more about V2 and any other V weapons which could be revealed. Suitably expanded, this would be precisely what the War Cabinet want on the subject of Crossbow."

NOVEMBER 1, 1945

A letter from the War Office objecting to any mention of the "large concrete structures at Mimoyecques was sent to Squadron Leader Vernon Noble of PR3. "We have to think of security that in the event of future trouble, these weapons might well be used against this country". Sqdn Ldr Noble sent this note to the Air Ministry.

"The Ministry of Information like the book as it is but are insistent that the full story of the rocket bombardment of London and of other V weapons which the enemy were preparing to launch should be included.

"We understand the War Office are reluctant to pass the details of the rocket guns.....Mr Cecil Day-Lewis of the publications division of the M of I says he understands that "the details of the Mimoyecques installations can be described and all the Chiefs of Staff ask is that there should be a formal security review of the text....

"The position is further complicated by the fact that Sqdn Ldr Bates is to be demobilised next week".

V-weapon — chronology of events

Here is a chronology of events from the time that the V2 rocket centre was opened at Peenemunde in 1937 to the landing on the moon in 1969. It will help readers to follow the progress of the Vengeance weapon campaign from its scientific beginnings, through 10 months of sheer terror and on to its peaceful and historic conclusion.

October, 1937: Rocket test centre at Peenemunde opened.

September 19, 1939: Hitler's first hint of "Germany's secret weapons".

June 9, 1942: Flying bomb idea becomes firm project.

June 13, 1942: First rocket test firing. It was a disaster.

October 3, 1942: Successful rocket test. Space travel is born.

December 24, 1942: First launching of a V1. Tests disappointing.

April 20, 1943: Duncan Sandys appointed supremo in hunt for secret weapons.

June 23, 1943: Rocket identified on photographs of Peenemunde.

August 17, 1943: Peenemunde bombed.

August 27, 1943: Suspicious construction in Pas de Calais bombed.

November, 1943: "Ski-sites" and flying bomb ramps identified by French secret agents.

December 16, 1943: Flt Lt. Cheshire leads night attack on "ski-sites".

May 16, 1944: Hitler's official order to attack England with flying bombs.

May 31, 1944: 82 V1 sites now neutralised by Allied Air Force.

June 13, 1944: First V1 (flying bomb) lands at Swanscombe, Kent. Another falls at Bethnal Green, killing 6 people.

June 15, 1944: Tempest Squadron established at Newchurch, Kent to lead battle in the air.

June 16, 1944: Flt Lt. Musgrave of 605 Squadron is first pilot to shoot down a flying bomb.

June 17, 1944: Bombardment begins in earnest. RAF lieutenant, interviewed by BBC, christens them doodlebugs!

June 18, 1944: 121 killed during Sunday service in Guards Chapel, Wellington Barracks, London.

June 19, 1944: Cabinet meeting. Churchill gives details of gun, searchlight and balloon defences.

June 20, 1944: Barrage balloon centre and "Diver" defence HQ established at Biggin Hill, Kent.

July 3, 1944: London evacuation begins. By July 17, 170,00 people have left capital. Numbers eventually grow to 1,450,000.

July 4-5: Raid on flying bomb storage depot at St Leu d'Esserent by 617 Squadron using Tallboy bomb.

July 5, 1944: Churchill tells House that 2,754 flying bombs have been launched and 2,752 people killed.

July 19, 1944: Anti-aircraft guns moved to coast. New defence plan established.

July 28, 1944: Flying bomb lands in market place at Lewisham. 59 killed.

August 4, 1944: First jet fighter, Gloster Meteor, joins battle. Dixie Dean of 616 Squadron tips over doodlebug with wing of aircraft. He is not the first pilot to try this trick.

August 23, 1944: Germans evacuate flying bomb sites.

September 8, 1944: "Mysterious" explosion on housing estate at Chiswick, killing three. More follow. Ministry calls them gas main explosions. It is, in fact, the long-range ballistic missile, the V2.

September 16, 1944: All flying bomb launching sites in France now captured. "Doodlebug alley" moves to Essex.

September 25, 1944: Rocket men driven further north. They set up shop in south-west Friesland.

October 15, 1944: Home Office makes decision to stand down Home Guard.

November 10, 1944: Churchill finally admits to V2 rocket. More than 100 already landed on London.

November 25, 1944: V2 explodes in New Cross and kills 160 — the worst V-weapon disaster of all.

December 24, 1944: Air-launched doodlebugs attack north of England.

March 27, 1945: Final rocket launched against England. It kills housewife in Orpington, Kent.

March 29, 1945: Final doodlebug lands on British soil. Explodes harmlessly in open country, near Sittingbourne, Kent.

May 2, 1945: Rocket scientists, Werner von Braun and Walter Dornberger surrender to Americans. They are taken back to States. Von Braun beomes naturalised American.

July 20, 1969: Von Braun, as head of Apollo Moon project, hears these words from Commander Neil Armstrong: "Tranquillity Base here. The Eagle has landed."

CHAPTER ONE

The thing that ain't quite human

ON the night of June 12th, 1944, six days after the invasion of France, there appeared over southern England a new object in the sky. It dashed northward like a flaming meteor over the rich hayfields and ripening cherry orchards of Kent, startled even the war-hardened citizens of that county into leaping out of bed and watching its fiery passage across the midsummer sky, caused a company of staid night-duty policemen at Maidstone to stand and cheer like schoolboys, under the mistaken impression that a German aircraft was on fire, and finally landed on a bridge at Bethnal Green, London.

Next morning the British public knew no more about it than it could read into a dry communiqué recording that a single enemy raider had been shot down over the London area. But in official places, in the War Office, Air Ministry, Home Office, in Intelligence rooms of those Commands responsible for the defence of Great Britain, there was full knowledge of what this object was, where it came from and what it could do. There was no illusion about the fact that this, at last, was the Hitler secret weapon, long trumpeted and long expected; the pilotless flying bomb, "the thing", as a Cockney lady afterwards commented, "that ain't quite human" — the Wellsian dream of robot flying power come true.

Three days later, this attack, itself only a range-finding affair of ten bombs accompanied by a discreet Junkers 88 for spotting, was followed by another salvo. It was bigger and more serious. Beginning in the early darkness of the evening of June 15th, it continued throughout the night. To the people of London and south-eastern England it looked like dive-bombing attacks had been made on a number of fast aircraft — and now they were all on fire. Contradictorily, it also appeared that they were all flying at a somewhat greater speed than the fastest fighter; and that their course ended always with an immense explosion.

The noise of their flight was hideous. It was coarser, louder, more blatant than the regular pulsation of ordinary aircraft, and was very like the clattering harshness of a cheap and gigantic motor bike. This ugliness of sound matched the appearance of "the thing", for which there was, as yet, no name.

In appearance it had, from below, the deathly crudity of a black cross; angular, simple, narrow, entirely without beauty. From the side it had something of the appearance of a giant rifle fitted with a telescopic sight. It flew at heights of between 2,000 and 3,000 feet and on a course from which there was no deviation.

It had been possible, and indeed desirable, to allow the first attack to remain secret. It had obviously been a trial affair. To mention it would give information to the enemy. But the second attack, consisting of 120 bombs flying in at five-minute intervals from points along 100 miles of coast, affecting thousands of people first in the countryside of Kent, Surrey and Sussex and then in the suburbs and centre of London itself, was quite a different thing.

In the first place, such an attack was obviously the beginning of a plan. It would be repeated. In the second place, the effect of an undescribed weapon, bringing with it the terror of the unknown, might conceivably shock civilian life and morale. It could scarcely be more of a shock, and would probably be much less if its purpose, effect and potentialities were immediately and frankly described.

Accordingly the next morning, June 16th, while every bus, tube, train, office, shop, home, pub and street corner in South East England was in a high state of fantastic speculation, Mr Herbert Morrison, the Home Secretary, made a statement in the House of Commons on the latest of man's scientific inhumanities to man.

He rose to address a House fully aware of the gravity of the position and said: "It has been known for some time that the enemy was making preparations for the use of pilotless aircraft against this country and he

Home Secretary, Mr Herbert Morrison (with glasses) visiting an Observer Corps in Kent, shortly after the first flying bombs were tracked.

This was Vergeltungswaffe 1 — Revenge Weapon No. 1 — the robot bomb designed to inject spirit into a fast-fading German national morale. Day after day, night after night it would speed across the sky, sometimes just above rooftop height. "In appearance it had, from below, the deathly crudity of a black cross; angular, simple, narrow, entirely without beauty."

has now started to use this much-vaunted new weapon. A small number of these missiles were used in the raids of Tuesday morning and their fall was scattered over a wide area; a larger number was used last night and this morning. On the first occasion they caused a few casualties, but the attack was light and the damage, on the whole, was inconsiderable. Last night's attack was more serious and I have not, as yet, full particulars of the casualties and damage, nor of the number of pilotless aircraft destroyed before they could explode. The enemy's preparations have not, of course, passed unnoticed and counter-measures have already been, and will continue to be, applied with full vigour. It is, however, probable that the attacks will continue and that, subject to experience, the usual siren warning will be given for such attacks.

"Meanwhile, it is important not to give the enemy any information which would help him in directing his shooting, by telling him where his missiles have landed. It may be difficult to distinguish these attacks from ordinary air raids and, therefore, it has been decided that, for the present, information published about air raids in southern England, that is, south of a line from the Wash to the Bristol Channel, will not give any indication where the air raid has taken place, beyond saying that it had occurred in southern England.

"All possible steps are, of course, being taken to frustrate the enemy's attempt to supplement his nuisance raiding, by means which do not imperil the lives of his pilots. Meanwhile, the nation should carry on with its normal business. As, however, the raids by pilotless aircraft may occur during daylight when the streets are full of people and anti-aircraft guns will be used to shoot down the machines, I must impress upon the public the importance of not exposing themselves unnecessarily to danger by remaining in the streets out of curiosity, instead of taking the nearest cover while the guns are firing."

The Home Secretary's statement had an immediate effect. It brought clearly before the British public, who were still watching with intense expectancy the course of the Armies on the Normandy beachheads, the simple facts of the position. This position was not pleasant. The prospects beyond it were not pleasant. Nor was any immediate respite from it promised. The people of southern England — which might have meant practically the whole of England south of

The first flying bomb was carefully plotted by the Royal Observer Corps on its journey, north-west across Kent. It crossed the coast at Dymchurch, flew on towards the county town of Maidstone and continued on its unerringly straight flight until the engine stopped near Gravesend. It dived to earth and exploded in open farmland, just north of the A2, at Swanscombe. The next day the Ministry of Home Security made a meticulous search of the area, gathering up all evidence that could be found. At that stage no general warning of the start of the new offensive was given.

This remarkable picture of a V1 flying over the Seven Sisters Cliffs and up the Cuckmere River Valley in Sussex was taken in the summer of 1944. Civilian photography of enemy war machines was strictly prohibited so the erstwhile photographer tucked it away in a family album where it has remained until now.

the Severn and the Thames but which, in fact, meant roughly a triangle formed by Dover, Southampton and London — found themselves caught up in a new and ugly situation. It was a situation in which the enemy, by the use of a robot weapon, could attack them night and day, wet or fine, as intensively as his resources would allow and for as long as his launching bases remained in his hands. It was clear that he hoped by this attack to discourage the British people in their determined prosecution of the war; to bruise and break their morale; and to cause them to demand such production of guns and fighters as would seriously affect operations in Normandy. In fact the counter attack to invasion was not to be, as had been expected, against the soldiers on the Normandy beaches, but against the common people of southern England. If the common people could stand firm while the soldiers in Normandy established themselves for successful battle, the enemy's hope would fail. That was the first and most important effect of Morrison's speech: the realisation by the people of these simple and unpleasant facts, and the determination to endure them and, if possible, conquer them. London was again in the front line.

The Home Secretary made no reference to London. The target area was vaguely defined as southern England and was so defined until, some weeks later, Mr Winston Churchill described it more precisely. Yet it would be well to realise that there was, from the beginning, only one main target: the largest metropolitan area in the world, twenty miles across, densely inhabited and congested, the home of nearly 8,000,000 people: London. Any target that was hit outside this huge area was an accidental target. With one or two exceptions, all the flying bomb bases in northern France were orientated towards London. The plan was, in its simplest physical terms, to blow London to hell — and not only to blow it to hell, but also to blow it to hell in revenge.

In Germany this was quite simply indicated by the name of the weapon. To all Germans the flying bomb was known as V1 — *Vergeltungswaffe 1,* Revenge Weapon No. 1. Its very name was a clear indication that it was not only a weapon of material power but also of propaganda power. It was meant not only to blast and discourage the enemy but to comfort and encourage the friend. Not the least of its objects was to inject spirit into a German national morale that had grown flabby under the long defeat from Alamein to Stalingrad and from Stalingrad to Normandy. It was the weapon of

"The Thing" which landed on top of the railway bridge at Bethnal Green in the early hours of the morning of June 13, 1944 was the first flying bomb to cause loss of life. Six people died, 30 were seriously injured and more than 200 were made homeless. This was the scene at Grove Road the following morning as bewildered firemen, Civil Defence workers and rescue teams speculated on the cause of so much devastation. Ten V1's were launched that night. Five crashed immediately, one came down in the sea and four crossed the Kent coast. The first plunged harmlessly in a field at Swanscombe at 4.13 am. The second crashed at Cuckfield in Sussex. The third hit the Grove Road bridge and the fourth came down at Platt near Sevenoaks. It was only a range-finding affair — but with it began the Battle of London.

By Friday and Saturday, June 16 and 17, flying bombs began to fall with unremitting frequency. Croydon, Wandsworth and Battersea were taking the brunt of the assault. Within one week, civilian casualties totalled 756 killed and 2,697 injured. Morrison helped to allay fears by saying the effect of the blast was no greater than that of a parachute mine, but every day there were reports of terrible casualties and vast damage.

hope, of "hang on a little longer and we will give you victory".

All this was clearly shown by the instantaneous reaction of the German press. It at once went mad with national excitement. It became a wild chorus of vehement gloating. The unpleasantly real situation in France, where Allied troops had made a mockery of Hitler's boast that they would never again remain on the continent of Europe, even for nine hours, was forgotten. In its place the lurid situation over England, part real, part mythical, aroused the German nation to a frenzied fever of hope. Goebbels, Germany's propaganda minister, announced: All London was on fire. The whole of southern England was covered with such a pall of smoke that it had not been possible to take photographs of the hideous shambles that obviously lay beneath them. North of London, where there was no smoke, the roads were seen to be choked with fleeing refugees even more terrified than those on the roads of Belgium and France in 1940. In London there were no public services; famous monuments and buildings were in ruins; the city was chaotic with panic and terror. If one day of flying bombs could do so much, what would ten do? What would a month of them do? What would three months of them do? The answer, for the German people, was that in three months the war would be won.

Comforted by such a desperate remedy in a desperate situation, the German people did not stop to ask themselves questions. They did not stop to ask where plans for the invasion of England had gone; plans similarly flaunted in the face of the world four years before. They did not ask after the disappearance of the Luftwaffe, their own air force, as an offensive power and no one, it seemed, was indiscreet enough to ask the Luftwaffe itself what it thought of a situation in which pilot-less aircraft were now preferred by the German High Command to aircraft piloted by men. Questions were

And what is a doodlebug? Punch

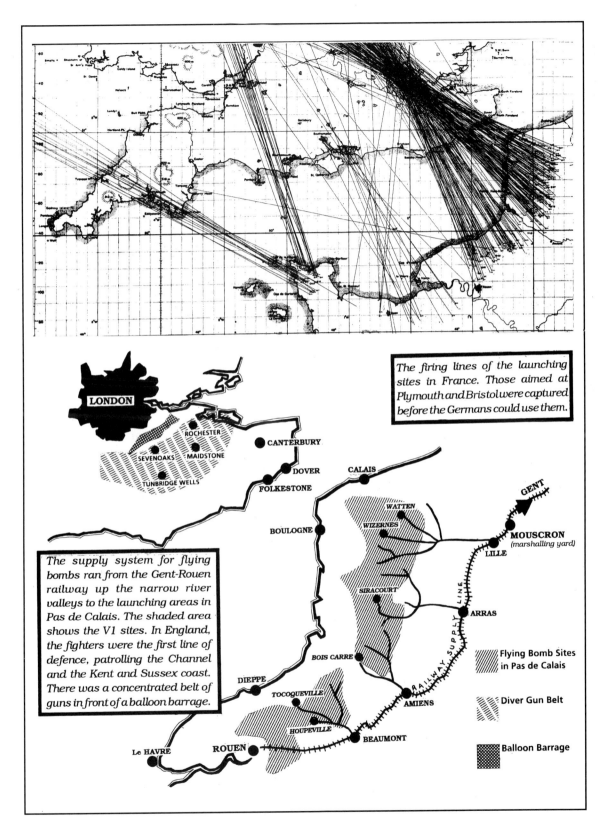

LONDON

ROCHESTER

SEVENOAKS   MAIDSTONE

TUNBRIDGE WELLS

CANTERBURY

DOVER

FOLKESTONE

CALAIS

BOULOGNE

WATTEN

WIZERNES

GENT

MOUSCRON
(marshalling yard)

LILLE

SIRACOURT

ARRAS

RAILWAY SUPPLY LINE

BOIS CARRE

DIEPPE

TOCQUEVILLE

AMIENS

HOUPEVILLE

BEAUMONT

Le HAVRE   ROUEN

The supply system for flying bombs ran from the Gent-Rouen railway up the narrow river valleys to the launching areas in Pas de Calais. The shaded area shows the V1 sites. In England, the fighters were the first line of defence, patrolling the Channel and the Kent and Sussex coast. There was a concentrated belt of guns in front of a balloon barrage.

Flying Bomb Sites
in Pas de Calais

Diver Gun Belt

Balloon Barrage

superfluous in a nation long since taught not to think for itself. On the German home front, so long-suffering, and equally on the Normandy battlefield, where Allied troops had already been established on occupied soil for nine days instead of nine hours, the German citizen and the German soldier thought alike, not only because they had been taught to think alike, but because there was no other way of thinking.

Both were equally sure that in a few weeks, at most in a few months, the new weapon could end the war. The businessman sleeping in his shelter in the Ruhr, the family in East Prussia waiting with terror for the approach of Russian armies, the prisoner captured in Normandy; all of them and millions like them had been taught to nurse the same blind faith in the new weapon.

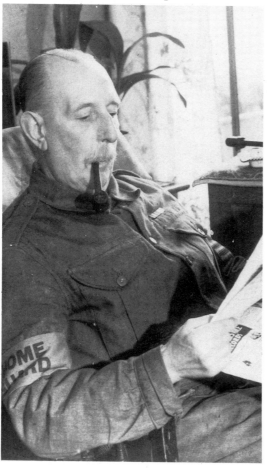

"London is chaotic with panic and terror. The roads are choked with fleeing refugees." Goebbels' words were far from the truth. The people of south-east England, and particularly London, were facing the new onslaught with a defiance that was now their hallmark. Here, a soldier of the Home Guard reads about Hitler's new miracle weapon and the destruction that it was causing. Civil Defence Controllers, Chief Constables, members of the Royal Observer Corps, ARP Wardens and the Home Guard were among the first to be given detailed information about the pilotless aircraft.

Mr Winston Churchill in the Cabinet Room of Number 10. "If the Germans believe that this attack will have the slightest effect on the course of the war or upon the resolve of the nation", he said, "they will only be making another of those psychological blunders for which they have so long been celebrated."

Dr R.V. Jones, scientific adviser to the Air Ministry was the man responsible for the early investigations into the feasibility of secret weapons. Various reports from underground units in occupied Europe and intelligence agents in Germany prompted him to write: "It is probable that the German Air Force has been developing a pilotless aircraft for long-range bombardment in competition with the Army rocket".

His summary of the available intelligence was accurate. The V1 was not discovered until the existence of the much more dangerous rockets had been proved. The uncovering of Germany's best-kept secret was one involving espionage, cloak and dagger operations, disagreement between scientists at the highest level and amazing scientific intelligence.

Duncan Sandys MP was appointed by Winston Churchill to take charge of a review of all the evidence for long-range rocket developments. His committee was called Bodyline, later to be changed to Crossbow. He initiated numerous photographic missions over France and Germany, worked closely with the interpreters and made inspection tours of Normandy. On June 27, 1943,

Sandys recommended the bombing of Peenemunde. It took a month of bitter argument before the War Cabinet agreed.

In November 1943 Sandys' responsibilities were tranferred to the Deputy Chiefs of Air Staff but a few days after the V1 offensive began he returned to chair the Crossbow Committee with wide powers to co-ordinate British counter measures.

The weapon was described as a Pilotless Aircraft or PAC in initial Ministry of Home Security reports. On June 19, 1944 the official name became Flying Bomb, abbreviated to FLY in daily summaries. To the people of South-East England it was The Thing, then a buzz bomb or doodlebug.

CHAPTER TWO

They called the thing a doodlebug

IT may be well, then, to take a look at this miracle weapon. We shall see later how it was launched from its bases in France, how it was attacked and shot down by fighters and guns, what damage it did, what effect it had on London and the English countryside, the people and the war. Meanwhile let us very briefly and as non-technically as possible, see what it really was.

Aerodynamically, the flying bomb was a small reaction-propelled mid-wing monoplane with a single fin and rudder. It had no pilot. The Germans have used two classes of it:

(A) Those controlled in flight by pre-set automatic pilots and usually launched from ground bases.

(B) Those guided on to their targets by means of radio controlled automatic pilots and usually carried into action by parent aircraft.

Those launched against England on June 12 and subsequently for about 80 days were of the first class. They consisted of a well streamlined fuselage, packed with a quantity of high explosive in the nose. To the fuselage were attached small wings, vertical and horizontal tail surfaces and a reaction propulsion unit — a true jet propulsion unit — mounted above the nose of the fuselage. The whole thing - a combination of missile and monoplane — was designed to explode on contact with earth and was of course expendable. It was controlled throughout its course by means of a pre-set automatic pilot.

More than one type of Class A flying bomb was subsequently put into service by the Germans against England but the type used in the first days of June had tapered wings of 16 feet span, with out-back wing tips. This version was succeeded by a type with wings that were slightly longer and with square cut tips. Its dimensions were:

Length of fuselage	*21ft 10ins*
Length of jet-propulsion unit	*11ft 3ins*
Overall length (including overhang of	
propulsion unit)	*25ft 4 ins*
Maximum diameter of fuselage	*2ft 8 ins*
Maximum diameter of propulsion unit	*1ft 10 ins*
Wing span	*17ft 6ins*

This special sectional drawing of the German flying bomb was published by the Illustrated London News in June 1944 and showed exactly how the robot's flight and dive was controlled. It cost 6d to buy a copy of the drawing and the proceeds were donated to the National Fire Service Benevolent Fund. The artist explained how the V1 was a pilotless mid-wing monoplane with a wing span of 17 feet 6 inches and an overall length of 25 feet 4 inches. It was constructed of thin sheet steel and plywood and easily produced in quantity. The

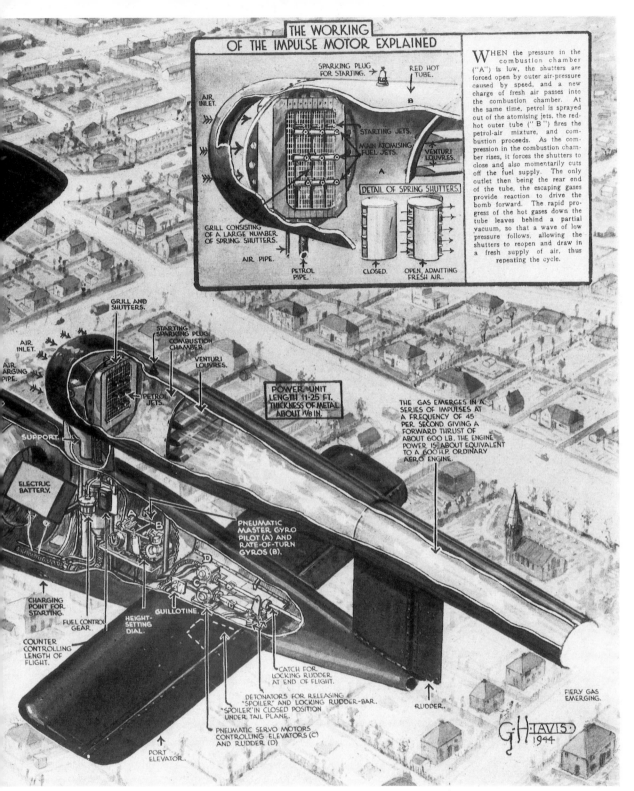

THE WORKING OF THE IMPULSE MOTOR EXPLAINED

WHEN the pressure in the combustion chamber ("A") is low, the shutters are forced open by outer air-pressure caused by speed, and a new charge of fresh air passes into the combustion chamber. At the same time, petrol is sprayed out of the atomising jets, the red-hot outer tube ("B") fires the petrol-air mixture, and combustion proceeds. As the compression in the combustion chamber rises, it forces the shutters to close and also momentarily cuts off the fuel supply. The only outlet then being the rear end of the tube, the escaping gases provide reaction to drive the bomb forward. The rapid progress of the hot gases down the tube leaves behind a partial vacuum, so that a wave of low pressure follows, allowing the shutters to reopen and draw in a fresh supply of air, thus repeating the cycle.

SPARKING PLUG FOR STARTING.

RED HOT TUBE.

AIR INLET.

STARTING JETS.

MAIN ATOMISING FUEL JETS.

VENTURI LOUVRES.

DETAIL OF SPRING SHUTTERS.

CLOSED.

OPEN, ADMITTING FRESH AIR.

GRILL CONSISTING OF A LARGE NUMBER OF SPRING SHUTTERS.

AIR PIPE.

PETROL PIPE.

GRILL AND SHUTTERS.

STARTING SPARKING PLUG

COMBUSTION CHAMBER.

VENTURI LOUVRES.

AIR INLET.

AIR CHARGING PIPE.

PETROL JETS.

POWER UNIT LENGTH 11·25 FT. THICKNESS OF METAL ABOUT ⅛ IN.

THE GAS EMERGES IN A SERIES OF IMPULSES AT A FREQUENCY OF 45 PER SECOND GIVING A FORWARD THRUST OF ABOUT 600 LB. THE ENGINE POWER IS ABOUT EQUIVALENT TO A 600 H.P. ORDINARY AERO ENGINE.

SUPPORT.

ELECTRIC BATTERY.

PNEUMATIC MASTER GYRO PILOT (A) AND RATE-OF-TURN GYROS (B).

CHARGING POINT FOR STARTING.

FUEL CONTROL GEAR.

GUILLOTINE.

HEIGHT-SETTING DIAL.

COUNTER CONTROLLING LENGTH OF FLIGHT.

CATCH FOR LOCKING RUDDER AT END OF FLIGHT.

DETONATORS FOR RELEASING "SPOILER" AND LOCKING RUDDER-BAR. "SPOILER" IN CLOSED POSITION UNDER TAIL PLANE.

PNEUMATIC SERVO MOTORS CONTROLLING ELEVATORS (C) AND RUDDER (D).

PORT ELEVATOR.

RUDDER.

FIERY GAS EMERGING.

G. H. DAVIS 1944

missile was propelled by a pulse jet engine using 150 gallons of petrol for fuel with compressed air as the oxidizer. The weapon had been designed so that the propeller-driven distance log automatically deflected the elevators to dive the bomb. The fuel supply was not cut off, as many thought. It was the sudden application of the negative 'G' force which caused fuel starvation, resulting in the engine cutting out. The silent dive to death was not intentional. The nose was armed with 850 kg of high explosive which was bolted to the fuel tank.

Its construction was of steel except for the fuselage nosecap, the elevators and the rudder, which were of light metal alloy. Fuselage, wings and tail surfaces were otherwise of sheet steel, in the form of stressed skin. The instruments of the control system and the automatic pilot alone were very complicated. The bomb compartment, or war-head, lay just behind the light metal alloy nose-cap and just forward of the leading edges of the wings , and was a steel casing about 2mm thick. It contained a charge of about 850 kg (1870 lbs) of high explosive and was therefore equal in weight to a bomb of about three-quarters of an English ton or almost the whole of an American ton.

Behind the war-head was a fuselage section. It contained a cylindrical fuel tank with a capacity of 150 gallons. This was roughly enough fuel for a journey of 130 miles. The power that made this journey possible came from a jet-propulsion of very simple, even elementary, design. It looked like a dustbin. A square grill took the place of the lid and a drumming stick stuck out of the other end. Its elementary construction was reflected in its primitively hideous noise as it fired and its efficiency in the high speeds it achieved in flight. Its directional control was governed by gyroscopics mounted in the rear of the fuselage and a pneumatic gyro-control system. The long flame of the exhaust gave to the whole ugly structure a fiendish kind of life.

At the end of its journey, the bomb began to dive. Its propulsion unit petered out through fuel starvation, the monoplane became soundless except for a strange and eerie rustling and, after an interval, sometimes very short, sometimes uncannily long, the bomb hit earth and exploded. This explosion was dynamic. Its effect was not downward, into earth, but outward , so that on all occasions the crater it made was astonishingly shallow and small in the immensity of its surface blast. Its noise could be heard at a great distance; its effect would be felt over miles.

The blast struck houses and large buildings and disintegrated them like a tornado against a house of straw. A single bomb could lay a country parish in ruins. It could blast the houses of a dozen London streets. It could make homeless, even if temporarily homeless, hundreds of people. It could blow the bodies of its victims into small pieces, far afield. In the lives of hundreds of people over its course and at its destination, it could not only kill but cause terror and misery and all the disheartening nuisances of disrupted life and homelessness.

A single bomb could lay a country parish in ruins. This is the scene of devastation caused by the doodlebug which fell in Snodland, Kent on August 5, 1944. Twelve died in this incident and 10 houses were completely demolished. Hundreds of homes were damaged in the blast.

They called the thing a "doodlebug"

"GOOD HEAVENS! WE CAN'T WIN A WAR THIS WAY!"

The flying bomb — the culmination of almost 50 years of experiments in aerodynamics — was in the Prime Minister's own words "science perverted to destruction". To the British people in the week ending June 17th it was largely an unknown thing. They knew that it flew and they knew that it exploded and they knew that it killed. They did not know how it flew or how it was launched or how it was guided and they had no name for it.

The British are an imaginative people and the functional German description V1, so typical of the Nazi and the regime, did not suit them. It is typical of the British and a tribute to the flexibility of English as a language that within twenty-four hours of their first heavy attack the name for the new terror had been found. Admirably, a Flight Lieutenant talking on the wireless, christened the weapon that had been simply "a thing"; and from that time onward all Britain knew it as the doodlebug.

ODDENTIFICATION

" Doodle Bug!"

CHAPTER THREE
Like Friday's footprint in the sand

ON the extreme north-western tip of the island of Usedom, off the Pomeranian coast of Germany, sheltered by the narrow neck of sea that broadens as it runs down to Stettin, lies a small village called Peenemunde. Pre-war editions of Baedeker had nothing to say of its importance even as a bathing resort; gazetteers gave the population as a few hundreds of people. To the British it was not even a name.

Early in 1943, however, the name of Peenemunde began to appear and recur more and more frequently in RAF secret intelligence reports. Before anything so definite even as a name was established, there had come in from British agents on the continent of Europe four rather vague reports which suggested that somewhere, at last, Germany was working in an experimental way on one of those secret weapons with whose potential terrors belligerent nations like to threaten each other. It was not known what this weapon was, except that it was a long-range weapon and of an unusual type. What was known, however, was that experiments, if there were any experiments at all, were being conducted on the Baltic coast. In the Spring of that year, therefore, photograph reconnaissance aircraft of the RAF began to spend a good deal of time there.

The first full-scale photographic cover of Peenemunde was commissioned on April 22, 1943. The place was so small that Baedeker had not even told the pre-war traveller whether he might buy himself a glass of beer there, but now very interesting things appeared to be happening. Among the sandy dunes of the sheltered neck of sea had sprung up what appeared to be quite a new town. Its many large buildings seemed to indicate that it had a good deal of importance and that it might in fact be a large experimental station. Experts of RAF Photographic Intelligence services were attracted and puzzled by Peenemunde. Its layout was very unusual; the plan of its buildings had many features not easy to explain.

Throughout the Spring of 1943 Peenemunde was photographed at frequent intervals and then examined for a clue. Finally the photographic experts discovered two large factories to the south-east of the site, an 'elliptical earthwork' to the south-west and, strangest of all, an object about 25 feet long projecting from the seaward end of the building. On a second photograph this object had disappeared and been replaced by a small puff of white steam.

Experts in England could offer no explanation of the earthworks, later identified as protective walls, so they ordered more photographic sorties. This time the interpreters discovered a cylindrical object and two white shapes, one of them a wagon. "Without doubt", said Sandys in his report to the War Cabinet, "Germany is developing a large rocket capable of bombarding an area from a very long range. Peenemunde must be bombed."

All this now seems quite simple. What can now be stated in a few words took several months of hard and specialised work to establish in the summer of 1943 so that gradually the jig-saw of Peenemunde became clearer. Facts that would help in its solution came from agents in Europe and by August it seemed clear beyond doubt that Peenemunde was no longer the harmless little seaside village left undescribed by the meticulous Baedeker. Its earthworks, its large buildings, its extensive water system, its plants that appeared to be designed for the production of hydrogen peroxide — all these obviously needed stronger attention than the aerial camera.

In August, accordingly, Peenemunde was bombed. Its relatively small target area, containing not only experimental plant and practical equipment but also the accommodation of some of Germany's important scientists, received the attention of Bomber Command on August 17/18. Aircraft dropped a load of 1,940 tons of bombs. There was extensive damage to workshops and experimental buildings and also to the living quarters that housed some of Germany's leading scientists. It is known that some of these scientists were killed.

The raid on Peenemunde had little to do with the V1 for the British did not know at the time that flying bomb trials were actually taking place on an airfield at Peenmunde West. As the area did not receive a single hit, the tests continued — but so did photographic reconnaissance. In November 1943, a young WAAF interpreter made a discovery that has some of the romance of Crusoe's discovery of Friday's footprint in the sand. She discovered in the sands of Peenemunde a tiny footprint in the shape of a cross. Magnified it looked like a miniature aircraft. To this exciting discovery, the vigilant interpreter added another. The little black aeroplane seemed

It was the RAF reconnaissance pilots of 540 Squadron who provided the first clear pictures of what was happening at Peenemunde. One showed a rocket lying on a road vehicle. Above it rose a massive observation tower and the steep encircling slope of elliptical earthworks. A later picture, taken in November 1943, showed a miniature aircraft at the end of a ramp in position for launching. The interpreter who made the great discovery was Flight Officer Constance Babington Smith, seen above with an enlargement of the famous photograph. She provided the link between Peenemunde and the launching sites in France. Hitler's "secret weapons" were no longer a secret.

to be sitting on a ramp. This ramp was inclined upward and appeared to be fitted with rails.

That was not all. Another photograph showed that the white sand about the ramp had been blackened. It was the sort of blackness that might have been caused by fire, still more likely by blast. The deduction was not difficult. It seemed very possible that the little aeroplane sitting on the ramp of steel rails was a robot machine that could not rise out of its own volition; that needed extraneous power to launch it; and that the blackening of the sand had been caused by the blast of that power.

Whether the robot aircraft was merely a target-plane of the Queen Bee type used in Britain before the war, or whether, in fact, it was an offensive weapon of a new and secret kind and linked in some mysterious way to the strange construction sites that had been sighted in Pas de Calais, no-one was certain. The interpreters sent their report to Duncan Sandys and his committee who established, without doubt, that the little robot was a flying bomb.

As the trials continued at Peenemunde, the intelligence agents were able to estimate roughly what the performance of a flying bomb would be. Its weight was assumed to be 8,000 lbs, its angle of climb thirty degrees, its cruising speed about 330 mph and its height in flight about 6,000 feet. Bearing in mind that these were figures for an experimental type, they were a most astonishingly accurate forecast of the weapon that finally emerged. We were aware also of the extent of its success.

The check point at the main entrance to Peenemunde. The security boundary ran from coast to coast across the airfield.

By December, 1943 failures at launching were still 39 per cent — but by the end of January, 1944 the Germans had accomplished the remarkable feat of reducing that to five per cent. During these trials it was estimated that 600 experimental bombs were fired and that the average of successful launchings was high

The attack by 600 aircraft of Bomber Command on the highly secret Research Station of Peenemunde during the night of August 17/18, 1943 was one of the most important and effective of the war. The destruction of the laboratories, workshops and administrative complex represented a severe check to the enemy's advance in the development of rockets. Ambitious plans by Hitler for a saturation onslaught were demolished at a single blow, for the Germans lost vital production time, estimated by some to be more than six months.

The attack was well planned and executed. The targets lay more than 600 miles from England and yet the first Pathfinder flares went down precisely on time and the show opened with a flood of light from the burning magnesium. The full moon flung the coastline into sharp relief.

A few hours later Peenemunde was burning. The scientific heart of the establishment was destroyed and there were direct hits on the assembly buildings where the V2 rocket was about to be mass produced. Tragically many bombs fell in the foreign workers' camp and the death toll among Polish labourers and Russian prisoners of war was appalling.

Peenemunde was rebuilt — but not immediately. The test firing of rockets was moved to Poland and mass production to vast underground caves.

Picture shows Test Stand V11 after the raid and the rails on which the rockets were moved.

enough to justify the belief that 60 per cent of all those launched in France would fall in the London area.

The production of the bomb and the building of the first launching sites — so-called ski-sites, named after the storage chambers built in the shape of a ski — was by now intensively in progress. The flying bomb, being expendable, was cheap to make and required only about one sixth or one eighth of the production effort that was going into the making of a single-engined fighter. Ski-sites could also be assembled fairly quickly. Up to mid-January the enemy was building them at an average rate of almost one a day. But as early as December heavy bombing had begun to affect that progress very considerably: so much so that repairs to severely damaged sites began to take as much as 22 days. Construction was severely curtailed. By the New Year the previous rate of progress was quite impossible to maintain and the enemy was forced to abandon the attempt to complete his first 100 sites and began to concentrate on the repair and construction of rather less than half of them.

In six months the combined forces of the RAF and the USAAF dropped a shattering weight on these targets. In December they dropped 3,217 tons; in January 6,726 tons; in February 5,532 tons; in March, 4,211 tons. With the coming of longer daylight and better spring weather in April, they dropped an average of about 650 tons a day, or about a ton every two minutes, making a total of 7,248 tons. By June, when the invasion began, they had dropped altogether 31,016 tons on ski-sites, supply sites, pre-fabricated sites and suspected rocket sites. In these six months seven large suspected rocket sites were in fact discovered in Northern France. At Mimoyecques, Tactical Air Forces dropped 550 tons in two attacks; at Siracourt they dropped 3,269 tons in 5 months. The percentage of the entire effort of the USAAF and the Tactical Air Force to be devoted to robot sites and bases in France is most impressive. Against the fact that great numbers of pre-invasion targets, notably the railways and bridges of France, also had to be remorselessly attacked if the invasion were to have any chance of success, the following figures are astonishing:

Amount of effort devoted to bombing robot sites and bases

	December 1943	*January 1944*	*April 1944*
Tactical Air Force	62.4%	90.1%	30.3%
USA 8th Air Force	13.9%	23.3%	17.5%

This is Siracourt, in Pas de Calais, where more than 3,000 tons of bombs were dropped in just over five months. Here, the reconnaissance photographers had spotted an ingenious construction which later turned out to be a huge store, outside the central doorway of which a large flying bomb launching ramp pointed ominously towards England.

Siracourt was to be one of the few fixed V-weapon structures which brought the Germans any return; it was incessantly bombed but the great bunker — more than 200 feet long — remained almost intact.

It was the Lancasters of 617 (Dambuster) Squadron, led by Wing Commander Leonard Cheshire, which were first given the task of destroying Siracourt and other 'ski-sites' where the flying bombs were stored. The mission to Siracourt was awesome; they dropped their bombs within 90 feet of the site but succeeded in rupturing only one section of the roof. The village itself was completely destroyed in this and subsequent raids but the inhabitants had all been evacuated.

As more 'ski-sites' were reported, bombers of the Allied Expeditionary Air Force joined in and by the end of May, 1944, 82 sites were believed to have been neutralised. The cost was heavy. The Allies lost 154 aircraft and 771 aircrew were dead or missing. This included 462 men of the US Eighth Air Force.

These attacks were pursued relentlessly, with what cost and what success we shall see precisely later, right up to the eve of D-Day. Exactly what they cost the enemy in wasted labour, materials and above all in time and lives it is hard to know. It is certain that it caused the abandonment entirely of the first type of site, the ski-site; great chaos in the elaborately planned supply sites; some of which had taken nearly two years to build and much damage to the later launching sites, some of which were never used. It is quite certain that it effectively delayed the enemy's attack for the critical six months before the invasion of Europe began.

Most of the evidence for pilotless aircraft and long range rockets was obtained by photographic reconnaissance. The Mosquito pilots flew long, lonely flights in their wooden aircraft over enemy territory in daylight and they developed techniques that were far in advance of any other nation's at the time. Unarmed, they relied on their speed — over 400 mph— to evade German fighters. There were hundreds of separate sorties yielding thousands of pictures, all of which were examined carefully by photographic interpreters. Many of the photocalls over Peenemunde in the summer of 1942 were made by Mosquito pilots of 540 Squadron, based at Leuchars on the east coast of Scotland. Tragically, six were to die within the next six months.

Group Captain John Searby (centre) with Squadron Leader John Manton (left) and Squadron Leader Ambrose Smith, Pathfinders with 83 Squadron. Manton and Smith led the early marking at Peenemunde, an exacting task which required great skill. Of these three men, Manton was to disappear with his crew and lose his life over Germany a few days later.

THE MASTER BOMBER

Group Captain John Searby, commanding 83 Squadron, was the Master Bomber chosen to lead the historic raid on Peenemunde, a technique pioneered by Guy Gibson on a raid of the Ruhr Dams. Searby had the highly dangerous and responsible task of controlling the operation from a flying command post right above the target area, radioing advice to his Pathfinders and then to the main force which consisted of 54 Squadrons of Bomber Command. Having waited for a full moon, the briefing took place with neither the briefers nor aircrew knowing what was at Peenemunde but they were told that the raid would have to be repeated every night until the job was done. It was achieved on Night One — a night of action and drama with many lives lost.

An entry from John Searby's diary of the dramatic "show" at Peenemunde.

Searby's logbook reads: "Master of Ceremonies. Night fighters accounted for many of our aircraft in bright moonlight. A good attack and resulted in the destruction of the Experimental Establishment. Attacked by T.E fighter and we claimed it as "damaged". Awarded immediate DSO.

The man who saved London

The reason that the ski-sites were so effectively knocked out by British bombers was largely due to the courage of French agents and it was the tenacity of two men in particular which forced Germany to abandon its initial plans to launch 5,000 flying bombs a month against London.

One was Michel Hollard (right) head of a resistance movement. The other was a young engineer called André Comps.

Hollard discovered the existence of the ski-sites after one of his team reported that he had heard two contractors discussing an unusual construction job. In order to find out for himself, he pushed a wheelbarrow onto the site at Bonnetot le Faubourg and

pretended to busy himself as a labourer. Hollard saw the strip of concrete and, consulting his pocket compass, noted that its orientation passed through London.

Comps went one better. He got a job with the Germans as a draughtsman and copied the plans of every building at the

Bois Carré site. One of the plans was actually removed from the coat of the German engineer supervising the construction.

Within three weeks, Hollard and his team — conducting their search principally by bicycle — had reported 60 sites near the Channel coast. By October, 1943, 100 sites had been identified. Their reports were sent to Dr. Jones, who then alerted Churchill to the threat they posed.

Hollard went on working until he was finally arrested by the Gestapo on February 5, 1944, He was atrociously tortured, including the "bath treatment" where he was submerged in a bath of cold water and violently beaten every time he put his head above water, so that he nearly drowned. The Gestapo failed to break him and sent him to a concentration camp. He survived and was finally liberated by the Allies.

Hollard became known as "the man who saved London". On the award of his DSO in 1945, the citation read: "Hollard, at great personal risk, reconnoitred a number of heavily guarded V1 sites and reported on them with such clarity that models were made which enabled effective bombing to be carried out".

A flying bomb falls on London behind the Law Courts.

CHAPTER FOUR

Boxers in a railway carriage

THERE seems very little doubt that the enemy meant to begin the use of V1 against England in the winter of 1943. The Luftwaffe had not then been superseded as an offensive force and it is very probable that the enemy plan was to use piloted bombers and unpiloted flying-bombs together, in fairly heavy strength, in pre-invasion attacks on London and the larger British ports.

The enemy knew quite well that invasion against him was being prepared; that its preparations would take time; and that many of these preparations, such as the assembly of shipping, could not be dispersed but had in fact to be concentrated. It was undoubtedly for this reason that several flying-bomb ramps in northern France were orientated not towards London but towards Bristol, Plymouth, Portsmouth and Southampton. These ports, like London, were inevitable invasion bases. To attack them in all weathers, night and day, throughout the winter of 1943-44, supplementing the attacks with raids by night bombers, might well have created serious obstacles to invasion plans.

The code name introduced by the Allies for flying bomb attacks was "Diver" and expert anticipation was that they would arrive at the rate of 200 bombs an hour. Any doubt as to whether the enemy could have sustained such a scale of attack for several months is removed when we see that 200 flying-bombs is an average train load; and that in France, at the much-bombed village of St Leu, no less than 37 train loads of flying-bombs were observed by local French intelligence to enter the storage caves in one day. Even this was only a small fraction of the storage potentialities of St Leu, of which we shall later hear much more.

The fact is that, although a double attack was expected, only a single attack came. The long and dynamic bombing of the north French coast, particularly of the Pas de Calais area where nothing more than military targets were ever specified, undoubtedly delayed the start of the robot offensive. Not only were the first 100 launching sites practically all destroyed, but a great many of the later types were, as we shall see, smashed to pieces in attacks by Bomber Command.

So the attacks against Britain in the early months of 1944 were made, thanks to twelve months intensive work of Secret Intelligence, Bomber Command and the USAAF, with piloted bombers only. And they were made at night. The Germans, in contrast to their raids in the winter of 1941, when attacks had lasted for as long as eight or ten hours, made their attacks amazingly short. By coming in over the east coast of Britain, turning south-east and gaining advantage of the prevalent north-west wind, they were able to bomb London and be away over the south coast in something like eight minutes. They flew at heights of between 27,000 and 30,000 feet. This height and the great speed at which they flew made contact very difficult for both night-fighters and anti-aircraft guns. While they lasted, these raids had power to annoy and hurt. But they were never of great weight and they did not last long. They petered out by April.

All this meant that preparations for invasion went practically unmolested; an amazing state of things in view of the fact that the enemy knew what was going on, that he still had the whole coastline of northern Europe in his hands and that he had bombing bases only a few minutes flying time away from the southern invasion ports, giving the defending forces there not more than a quarter of an hour's warning of attack. But it gave us another advantage. It meant also that our preparations for flying-bomb defences were given more time. These preparations were complicated. They were co-ordinated under the Command of Air Marshal Sir Roderick Hill, Air Officer Commanding that part of the RAF known for the period of invasion operations as Air Defence of Great Britain (ADGB), formerly known as Fighter Command. This change in the organisation of the Command had been made necessary by the tactical needs of invasion plans. Air defence of the country had now to be completely separated from offensive operations over the Continent. For this purpose the Tactical Air Force (TAF) was created and Fighter Command re-formed and given another name. In controlling the machinery for the defence of Great Britain, ADGB not only had at its disposal the forces of the RAF, but also those of AA Command under the leadership of Sir Frederick Pile. It controlled also Balloon Command, the RAF Regiment and the Royal Observer Corps; it was responsible for the Raid Reporting System. Linked with the plan were the vast organisations of Civil Defence, the National Fire Service, railways, police, hospitals, Women's

When the 59th Surrey Battalion of the Home Guard was disbanded, the gunners quickly reformed to man the 4.5inch anti-aircraft guns at Shirley Park Golf Club. Then the flying bombs began to appear and the men on the AA batteries in South London could not believe their luck. The targets, flying a straight course with a flaring exhaust, were so enticing that the gunners fired wildly in the air and cheered madly when the cut-out by the engine seemed to indicate a score. It was some time before they realised they were bringing the missile down on to the very target at which it was aimed.

Voluntary Service, Home Guards, evacuation, health and housing authorities.

When, therefore, the flying bomb attack began in June there was already in existence an extensive plan to meet it. It was a plan that had to be altered and, in one respect, drastically altered as the attack went on. But in original conception, so far as active defence went, it was this: along the southern and south-eastern outskirts of London a balloon barrage, sited mostly along the North Downs in order to gain height; beyond this a belt of AA guns; and beyond this a zone of fighters.

Now all this seems simple. In theory the first belt of fighters would attack the flying-bombs as they came over the sea, the coast and the first twenty miles or so of Kent and Sussex; the bombs that succeeded in getting clear of fighters would be attacked by guns, sited broadly along the heart of the two counties and those that evaded the guns would be faced by balloons, lined between Gravesend and Biggin Hill.

But it was not at all as simple as this. For though offensive bombing had so reduced the enemy's potential that he could now hope to send only about 200 bombs per day instead of 200 bombs an hour, the defence problem was severe. The doodlebug could travel at six miles a minute. From launching site to target — in this case Metropolitan London — took only 20 minutes. This gave defences not more than 15 minutes clear warning. And from the coast to London was only 10 to 12 minutes flying time.

Time and space — as in the piloted bomber attacks of the early year — were therefore greatly in the enemy's favour. The problem of deploying the defences in such a restricted area and restricted also by time — was consequently most acute. A fighter having a clear run from Calais to Westminster, a distance of 90 miles, would find that his small overtaking speed would be hardly enough to give him time to make an interception. But his run in reality was only 45 miles. Guns and balloons occupied the rest. The guns needed time to shoot and their ideal condition of engagement required a clear belt of 15,000 yards wide if they were not to be forced to hold their fire for fear of hitting our own aircraft. Finally the balloons had to be so far forward as to avoid impacted bombs overshooting into the suburbs of London itself.

All this has been described as rather like having two or three boxing matches in a crowded railway carriage. Several people wanted to fight

A flying bomb has been spotted and, at a command post, the telephonist shows the flight commander the approach of the bomb on the squared map. Above ground, the spotter, Leading Aircraftsman Harvey of Pendlebury, sounds the alarm.

without having room to fight. Nor was the problem only a linear one. The anticipated flying height of the doodlebug was up to 7,000 feet. In practice it came over at 2,000 to 3,000 feet. This still further compressed the whole problem. It brought the ceiling of the railway carriage down, so to speak, so that it was hard for the boxers to swing their arms. It was equally hard for them to avoid hitting friend as well as foe.

Before we see how these problems were tackled, let us look at the doodlebug again. We anticipated as early as December, 1943 that it would have the following characteristics:-

Construction: *Jet-propelled monoplane of 19 or 20 feet, taking off from ground installations.*

Range: *130 miles at from 500 to 7,000 feet.*

Speed: *Variable: between 250mph to 420mph.*

Control: *Magnetic in gyroscopic warhead: up to one ton.*

Compare these figures with those already given. They are remarkably accurate. To this excellent information we were able to add several other things. The doodlebug, being non-human, flew on a fixed and level court. It took no evasive action. Its speed did not vary in flight. It knew nothing of tactics. It could not fight for itself. After a time, AA experts realised that just as in ordinary air combat, the human element governs the mechanical, so in flying bomb attacks the aim was to have a robot defence against a robot target: realisation of an utterly Wellsian idea.

Defence therefore was ready. In the Fighter Zone it consisted of six Spitfire and two Tempest Squadrons based at airfields in Kent. Overall control of all "Diver" defences was given to Biggin Hill Operations, which in 1944 was situated at a large house called Towerfields.

The aircraft were to operate by day and by night in co-operation with searchlights, the deployment of which had been thickened to a spacing of 3,000 yards.

In the AA zone, south of the North Downs, extending across some miles of country, there were four rows of eight-gun batteries, each row 3,000 yards apart, each gun site spaced laterally 6,000 yards from its

The corporal of a balloon crew paints two flying bomb symbols on the envelope. The cable brought down two doodlebugs in successive days.

neighbour. On each of these sites, as well as on each of the searchlight sites, there was also a 40mm gun. All this involved, as the campaign opened, more than 1,000 guns. They were operated by 18 regiments of AA Command — girls and men — supplemented by 14 regiments drawn from the 21st Army Group and Home Forces, further supplemented by 30 Squadrons of the RAF Regiment.

Behind this gun zone was the only materially beautiful thing produced by the whole campaign: the balloons. The sight of up to two thousand of them glowing in the southern sun, smooth and silver against the blue sky, was at all times an incongruous thing in this odd campaign of hideous robot combat.

All this deployment of aircraft, guns and balloons, which could be seen and heard by the public night and day, was backed by the Royal Observer Corps, whose job it was, as always, to plot anything that flew, friendly or enemy, robot or piloted and itself to remain out of sight.

This is the plan, therefore, that went into action in the week of June 11-17, in spite of the fact that a far larger plan, the largest in all military history, involving a huge diversionary deployment of guns, ships, aircraft and men, had also been put into operation only ten days before.

It has been said that all military plans of campaign become obsolete the moment the campaign begins. This half-truth is another way of saying that any military plan is conditional. Its success or failure depend on conditions that cannot be foreseen: the weather, the enemy's reaction, the enemy's strength, the element of human behaviour. All plans are based, to some extent, on surmise.

So with the flying bomb. Its exact characteristics, its speed, its height, its density of attack, were things that could only be intelligently guessed. As events turned out, predictions were remarkably good. The average speed of the bomb turned out to be 350-450mph, and its height between 2,000 and 3,000 feet, with occasional variations below and above that level.

But the weather could not be predicted at all. Whatever it was, it was evident that it would profoundly affect the plan of defence. The flying bomb could fly in all weathers, and it was very probable that the heaviest attacks would come in the worst weather. Since both fighters and guns relied on good weather to make their interceptions, it was likely that the heaviest attacks would be the most successful. It was

Once it was certain that Hitler's secret weapons were a reality, the balloon barrage went up. A great, glistening, formidable wall of some 1,750 balloons floated over the North Downs from Cobham in Kent to Limpsfield in Surrey, with the fighter station, RAF Biggin Hill also becoming the Balloon Centre. It was the duty of the balloon squadrons to select the sites for emplacements while the Airfield Construction Wing built access roads, hard standings, centre anchorages and hydrogen depots. The airmen were responsible for the handling of balloons while WAAFs managed the transport, collected the heavy cylinders of hydrogen and delivered food rations to the sites. With later extensions the balloons covered 260 square miles of countryside.

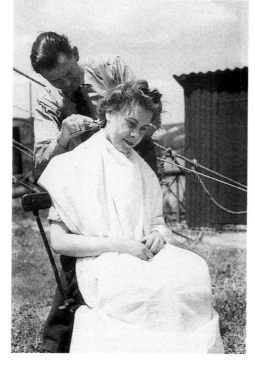

Scores of Balloon Squadrons arrived in Kent on July 16, 1944 and set up camp at Biggin Hill. They came from all over England including Liverpool, South Wales and even Scotland. Here, a WAAF from Manchester has a haircut in the open-air barber's shop at Balloon HQ.

therefore arranged that under the clearest weather conditions fighters should have full freedom and the guns should close down. In average weather fighters would be allowed to chase bombs across the gun belt and up to the balloon line. In thick weather, if patrols could still be maintained, fighters would keep clear of the gun belt and allow the guns full freedom of action up to 8,000 feet. These three conditions were rather comically known as *Flabby, Fickle* and *Spouse.*

Defence, therefore, was governed by the weather. And the weather could hardly have been worse. Twelve days after the invasion of the Continent, both England and north-western Europe were hit by the worst June gale for forty years. From this extraordinary event the summer never recovered. June was cold and wet; July was if possible colder and wetter; August recovered a little but after a heatwave became worse than July; September was worse than August and October far worse than September. It was the earliest and wettest autumn within living memory.

In all conditions, the pursuing fighter had only five or six minutes in which to make its interception between the coast and the balloon line. But in *Fickle* conditions this was hopelessly reduced and complicated by guns and fighters mutually interfering with each other. Across the middle of Kent and Sussex, in fact, the noise of fighters, guns and bombs was, under these conditions, an almost continuous crazy chaos. When *Spouse* conditions came, the main work fell on guns and balloons. But balloons found themselves very often hampered by static electricity and the sole defence was then with the guns.

Front-line farm girls plough close to a balloon site on the North Downs in Kent.

CHAPTER FIVE

The worst sound of all was silence

UNFORTUNATELY, in those early days, all was not well with the guns. On the morning of 16th June, Anti-Aircraft Command had learned, with some dismay, that the height of the flying bombs was between 2,000 and 3,000 feet. This meant that they were above the effective maximum height for light AA guns and too low for satisfactory radar pick-up for heavy.

Two officers of the Command were immediately sent on a tour of the gun sites in London, East Kent and the South Coast. They remained away from 16th June until late evening of the 18th and wherever they went they found their worst fears justified. The shooting, in their own words, was wild and inaccurate. The tough little flying bomb seemed an almost hopeless target for AA guns. Its smallness, its speed and its comparatively low level all far outweighed the fact of its straight flight and its lack of evasive action. The guns were also poorly sited, with both bad visual and bad radar view. All the heavy AA sites were in hollows: a quite useless radar situation against such low targets. As the tops of hills would have been equally bad it was very difficult to know what change to make. It was clear that rapid and radical changes had to be made.

By Sunday June 18th a report on these changes was ready. By Monday 19th it was submitted to the GOC, General Sir Frederick Pile and by the evening of that day it had been discussed and adopted. It provided for:

(a) a new training plan

(b) the provision of drills and instructions

(c) the provision of new equipment

(d) the provision of instructors to carry out retraining on the new equipment

and most important,

(e) the entire re-deployment of guns to sites having a better visual and a better radar view on the coast.

Now, to move so many guns, so much ammunition, so many officers and men, and so much equipment of all kinds was in itself a revolutionary thing. AA Command purported to be a static Command.

It had not been conceived or designed for sudden large moves about the country. The decision to make such an enormous move entailed vast re-organisation of all kinds. To move practically an entire Command and also at the same time train it in the use of equipment it had never seen before was a prodigious task. Yet it was accomplished in exactly one month from the day on which two tired officers had returned to London with their first report. The immensity of the whole task may be seen from the fact that in one week:

Vehicles of all sorts covered 2,749,500 miles

8,000 lorries were detailed

30,000 tons of stores lifted

9,000 RASC personnel employed; and over 1,000,000 rounds of heavy AA shells were moved into the coastal area.

All this time intensive re-training in new American equipment was going on. This equipment had been personally requested by Mr Churchill in December 1943, had been instantly promised by Mr Roosevelt and had begun to arrive in June. The feat of re-training an army in the use of new equipment while that army was actually engaging the enemy on the site of battle was something never attempted by an army before. To this problem had to be added another; the establishment of AA Command was not enough to allow every gun to be manned for 24 hours at a time. Yet the fact that the flying bomb was a 24-hour-a-day menace and that its approach in all weather gave so short a warning meant that guns had in fact to be manned for every hour of the day. Great numbers of extra troops had, therefore, to be drafted from remote parts of the country to the south coast. The responsibility of these troops at their original stations was taken over by the Home Guard.

By July 17th, therefore, all the newly sited batteries were in position on the south coast. Two days later the light batteries followed them. These changes were only part of the entire re-alignment of the defences of the Air Marshal Commanding ADGB, Roderick Hill. With the guns now sited all along the coast from South Foreland to Beachy Head the area of fighter patrol had also to be altered. The first fighters now patrolled out to sea, but did not cross the coastal gun belt in their chase. The second belt of fighters took up the chase inland, beyond the guns, and carried it up to the balloon belt on the North Downs. In this way the guns, now static and remote controlled with

This battery of guns on Romney Marsh in Kent, one of hundreds both British and American, contributed to the barrage which destroyed so many doodlebugs. It was in the area between Hythe and Rye where the greatest number of guns was assembled and thousands of homes in the area were damaged by falling shells, some of which hit their target and bounced off causing more damage on land. As the campaign progressed, however, the gunners became more and more accurate and by August 23rd the percentage of "kills" had risen to 60 per cent. In the last week of this phase of the battle it rose to 74 per cent.

automatic laying instead of being mobile and laid by hand, had an uninterrupted view of their targets. They were able to traverse very rapidly, in a way that could not be done by hand, and they were no longer hampered by fighters.

We now had many more fighters. The new Tempest, carefully guarded and spoken of in whispers, appeared both by night and by day. The squadrons increased to:

3 Tempest squadrons

4 Spitfire XIV squadrons

4 Mustang squadrons

2 Spitfire LF squadrons

1 Spitfire XII squadron

By the end of July every schoolboy and farm labourer in Kent and Sussex was delighted also by the appearance of an entirely new aircraft, smooth and fast, that flew with the sound of an immense and continuous whisper, trailing faint double exhausts but having no propellers: subsequently revealed as the Gloster Meteor, the first British jet-propelled fighter.

This was only one of the many excitements of south-eastern England. The life of the summer was rapidly becoming something of a nightmare. If in America the doodlebug remained for some time a subject for cartoons and in the rest of England little more than the subject of a stereotyped communiqué, it was because hardly anyone there knew what the doodlebug looked like or sounded like, or what a man's emotions were as he heard and watched an entirely robot aeroplane roaring like a harsh and hideous express train across the sky. And a man's emotions were not pleasant. The doodlebug could be heard from a long way off. It came out of the clear summer distance or out of the rain or the dark July cloud with a low level roar that could be heard about thirty miles away. It seemed to fly on an invisible track, as straight as a train. As it came nearer the roar became a metallic throb like the fiery stroke of a cheap motorbike and, as it passed overhead these throbs set up the most deafening reverberations that were like the explosion of a continuous backfire.

And since the enemy's favourite tactics were to launch the bombs in salvoes they rarely came singly. As many as half a dozen would come roaring over together on parallel tracks separated by about a mile. The noise was fantastic. Crows in the fields rose up with their

Evening Standard

37,383   BLACK-OUT: 11.3 pm—5.7 am   MOON: Rises 10.42 pm; Sets 7.7 am   ONE PENNY

Mr. Churchill Tells Story of Flying Bombs, Says Our 50,000 Ton Attacks Saved London Six Months of Bombardment

2754 BOMBS LAUNCHED— OUR DEATH ROLL IS 2752

100 Bases Were Wiped Out, But Enemy Built New Ones

"London will never be conquered, and will never fail in her renown. Triumphing over every ordeal, her light will long shine among men."—Mr. CHURCHILL to-day.

Up to 6 a.m. to-day 2754 bombs have been launched at this country. They have killed 2752 people—"almost exactly one person per bomb"—and are being discharged at a rate of between 100 and 150 a day.

THIS WAS REVEALED BY MR. CHURCHILL WHEN HE MADE HIS STATEMENT ON THE FLYING BOMBS IN PARLIAMENT TO-DAY.

He announced that 8000 injured people had been detained in hospitals—not counting minor injuries—and that a little over 10,000 of the total casualties, severe or mortal, had been in London.

Our bombers have dropped 50,000 tons of bombs on flying bomb and rocket targets, and have destroyed about 100 of the enemy's smaller sites between Le Havre and Calais.

"If it had not been for bombing operations on France and Germany," said the Prime Minister, "the bombardment of London would no doubt have started perhaps six months earlier, and on a very much heavier scale."

TO USE DEEP SHELTERS

Answering a question he said it had now been decided to make use of deep shelters which had always been regarded as a reserve. With regard to evacuation, the aged and infirm must be considered, but the children came first.

Mr. Churchill said:

I consider that the Government were right in not giving a great deal of information about the flying bomb until we knew more about it and were able to measure its effect.

The newspapers have, in an admirable manner, helped the Government and I express my thanks to them.

The time has come, however, when a fuller account is required, and a wider field of discussion should be opened. In my view such a discussion is no longer hampered by the general interest.

Be Careful!

I would, at the same time, enjoin on the House and on the public to watch their step in anything they say; because a thing which might not strike one as being harmful at all might give some information to the enemy which would be of use to him and a detriment to us.

Still, a very wide field of discussion will be open henceforward.

Let me say at the outset that it would be a mistake to under-rate the serious character of this particular form of attack. Cer-

The Choice That Faces Germany

Mr. Attlee, Deputy Prime Minister, told the Commons to-day:

So far as the Government is concerned, it has repeatedly been made clear in public statements that we shall fight on until Germany is forced to capitulate, until Nazism is extirpated, and it is for the German people to draw the logical conclusion.

He was replying to Mr. Rhys Davies (Soc., Westhoughton), who asked the Prime Minister whether consideration had at any time been given by the Government, or its Allies, to the advisability of informing the German people that if the present Nazi Government were displaced, and a democratic regime emerged in the Reich in which the Allies could have faith, the way would be opened for an approach towards a settlement on the basis of principles of the Atlantic Charter.

Mr. Attlee added: "If any section wishes to see a return to a regime based on rule by international law and the rights of the individual, they must understand that no one will believe them until they themselves have taken active steps to rid themselves of the present regime.

"The longer they continue to support and tolerate their present rulers, the heavier grows their own direct responsibility for the destruction wrought throughout the world and not least within their own country."

Mr. Rhys Davies—Do I take it that the British Government and the Allies would not be unwilling for an approach to a settlement if this conflict with a democratically minded government, and will not the Government take the lead, with all its power and experience of diplomacy, to relieve mankind?

Mr. Attlee—The Government's

THE DEEP SHELTERS: "NOT FOR FEW DAYS"

It was stated this afternoon by the Ministry of Home Security that the deep shelters to which Mr. Churchill referred in his reply to a Parliamentary question to-day will not be open for a few days.

Summer in The Straits

It was summer weather in the Straits of Dover to-day. At noon the temperature was 73 degrees in the shade, having risen 5 degrees since 8.30.

The thermometer was still rising. The sun streamed down from a cloudless blue sky and there was only a light southerly breeze. The barometer was steady. The sea was very calm and visibility

AIR BLOWS MOUNT

"Nothing Like It Before"

"Nothing like it has been seen or heard on this part of the Kent coast before," said one observer to-day after four great forces of aircraft had roared out within a few hours.

They were going out from midnight to breakfast time in "masses which blackened the sky."

And here are their objectives:

During the night R.A.F. bombers attacked the flying bomb installations and other military objectives in Northern France in strength. Squadrons of Mosquitoes attacked a synthetic oil plant at Buer-Scnolven, near Gelsenkirchen, Germany, and other targets in the Ruhr. Mines were laid and six aircraft were lost.

R.A.F. Lancasters made a deep night penetration through fighter defended areas in France to attack the railway marshalling yards at Dijon.

This was to block yet another route which the Germans, faced with the disorganisation on the railways farther north, could use to bring supplies and reinforcements from Germany by a long detour towards the battlefield.

A great weight of high explosive bombs was dropped.

Supporting the American advance down the Cherbourg Peninsula, Mosquitoes went out last night to attack railways, road junctions and encampments in woods behind the German lines. Targets were at Villedieu, Hyenville and Granville.

"Wolf Packs" of the Air

Wolf packs" of German fighters, operating on similar lines to the U-boats, are now operating in the Normandy battle zone, says Ian Munro, Reuter's correspondent at Shaef.

(Continued on Back Page, Col. Three)

CANADIANS IN "HOT SPOT" HOLD FAST

THE BATTLE FOR CARPIQUET HAS TEMPORARILY ENDED WITH GERMAN AND CANADIANS SHARING THE PITCH WITH THE GERMANS AT THE THREE-QUARTERS LINE, SAYS DOON CAMPBELL, REUTER CORRESPONDENT WITH THE BRITISH FORCES, IN A DESPATCH FROM NORMANDY TO-DAY.

The Canadians in the Carpiquet hot spot have not budged, adds Ross Campbell, Reuter and Canadian Press correspondent.

"Rations and ammunition are going up to them all right, despite the shelling and mortaring of the approaches to the village.

About ten German tanks were knocked out by the Canadians during the four attempted counter-attacks yesterday morning, but the Germans still have 500 and 600 troops, supported by artillery and mortars, on the immediate Carpiquet sector.

To-day's Allied communiqué says: "Our positions at Carpiquet have been held. Enemy attacks continue."

LINE PACKED

Rommel has massed so many troops along the Tilly-Caen front that saturation point has been reached where the fighting is fiercest, says a reported at Supreme Headquarters.

At these hot spots there is a concentration practically unsurpassed even in the last war. Rommel can pack in no more men.

Already at some parts of the line Rommel has one division to less than three miles.

INTENSE FIGHTING

The Canadians have been involved in fighting as intense as anything the Allies have experienced anywhere.

The German reaction to the

(Continued on Back Page, Col. Four)

Hitler Throws In Reserves

Hitler is reported to have ordered his generals to hurl in all their reserves against the Russians.

According to a Stockholm report, quoted by Moscow radio, General Kurt Zeitzler, chief of the German General Staff, visited Hitler to tell him that the German army were faced with a superiority which they could not match.

These reserves—some have already been thrown in—will have to face an onslaught which is sweeping everything before it along a 400-mile front.

The Red Army are to-day 120 miles from the East Prussian border, cables Duncan Hooper, Reuter's correspondent.

The Germans have thrown in flame-throwing tanks in an attempt to hold up the Soviet advance, but the Russians are steamrolling nearer to Vilna, the capture of which would sever the direct railway links between the German groupings in the north and those in the centre and the south.

The German front has now broken up into three main salients —north of Smorgon, on the route to Vilna, west of Minsk, and from a point 82 miles south of Minsk to Turov on the Pripet.

The Germans will have to abandon further territory, and they are already about to do so, said Martin Hallensleben, chief correspondent of the official German news agency to-day.

88mm. Gun Captured at La Haye

E-Boats Tried

---

own terrified explosion of wings and in houses dogs and cats cowered in their secret places for shelter. People who had never been frightened by the sound of a bomb or a bomber found themselves nervous at the roar of the doodlebug.

If the noise of it travelling was bad enough, its sudden silence was worse. That sudden silence meant that somewhere, sooner or later, the bomb was coming down. Sometimes a bomb was hit by guns or fighters over the coast and floated silently inland for some miles before falling. Sometimes it tilted into a steep dive and went straight to earth. Sometimes the engine in the gyroscopic control did not seem to be working normally and the bomb came along at slower speed, coughing and missing its strokes and picking them up again, or sailing crazily round the countryside on what seemed to be an elliptical course. Frequently, and in fact very frequently from the middle of July, it appeared with as many as half a dozen fighters in pursuit, rather like so many young dogs chasing an electric hare.

The golden wink of their guns in the wings could be seen a few seconds before the sound of them could be heard. If you were directly below them it was a moment of tense and terrifying beauty. For the impact of the shells on the bomb came at about the same moment as

With all the activity going on overhead, tin hats became the order of the day for all those working in the open during this frantic phase of "doodlebuggery". The missiles were crashing with unremitting frequency into the fields of Kent and Sussex.

With their eyes trained on the skies and their ears tuned in to that tell-tale low-level roar, the people of doodlebug alley continued with their everyday work. Londoners had their own spotters and alarm systems including bells, flashing red lights and vocal warnings which reached fever pitch when the engine of the flying bomb abruptly stopped. Schools in Kent and Sussex also refused to trust the official air-raid warning and tin-hatted children took it in turns to stand in the playground and shout "doodlebug" whenever one appeared. This photograph taken in July 1944 shows Pamela Sturmer and Rosemary Watson of Otham School, near Maidstone doing their stint of doodlebug spotting.

the shells being fired, and in the few seconds of interval you could only wait with breathless and uncertain excitement. If there was no impact and the bomb was not hit you knew that it would fly on until the fighter attacked it again and you knew, not without a certain natural human relief, that for the moment you were safe again. You knew too that it would go on until it was forced down or came down of its own accord, and that wherever it came down, the lives of innocent and decent people would be terrorised or blown into a thousand unrecognisable pieces. If, on the other hand, the bomb was hit and the fighters turned suddenly and steeply away, you had two chances. There was a chance, and it was a good chance, that the bomb would burst in the air, exploding into countless pieces that did nothing more than frighten the birds, the blast of it simply absorbed by the spaces of sky. Or there was a chance that if it came down the bomb would fall harmlessly in woods or fields, hurting nothing but a sheep or two, and since the English countryside is not so thickly populated as statisticians sometimes seek to show, that was a good chance too.

All this happened by day; and it happened also, with some differences, at night. By day the people of Kent and Sussex could stop their work in hayfields or cherry-orchard or shop or factory, or wherever it was and calculate the behaviour of the bomb by what they could see and hear. At night it was rather different. Every night an air-raid warning sounded as darkness fell, whether in fact bombs were approaching or not. In this way the population of London and the south-east was told that they were expected to try to rest if they could. Very sensibly the

"There is no weak link."

greater part of the population went to bed, but if you lived in that part of the countryside that became known as doodlebug alley, going to bed was a curious experience. When bombs came you had, as in the daytime, two chances. You could get out of bed and into shelter; or you could stay in bed and hope. Hoping, curiously enough, was the chance that thousands and thousands of sturdy English

A tin-hatted, overalled clergyman, grey with the dust of wreckage, stops for a smoke and a chat during his rescue work among the homes of his parishioners. In London the citizen only had one chance. He knew that the bomb must fall there. He knew it was intended for him.

country citizens took every night for about eighty nights in the summer. They lay in bed and listened to the bombs travelling up on their courses from the coast; they listened to the sound of night-fighters firing; and they listened too for the worst sound of all: the sound of silence. And in that miserable, taut, uncertain existence they were very brave.

The people of doodlebug alley were in fact never free. In eighty days and nights they had every chance to see and hear practically everything a flying bomb could do. They saw it fall on their ancient and beloved churches, on schools and hospitals, on some of the loveliest villages, not only in England but in the world. They saw the monuments and landmarks of centuries go down in dust. They never knew from one moment to another whether the meal they were eating, the glass of beer they were drinking, or the dart they held poised in their hand ready to throw at the saloon-bar board might not be their last. They said goodbye to their children as they went to school in the morning and never knew if they would see them again. The Battle of Britain, which they had been thrilled and proud to see with their own eyes in the glorious summer days of 1940, was a memory without fear. The Battle of the Doodlebug, if ever they thought of it like that, was a time entirely without thrill or pride. They hated it; the edges of their nerves were rubbed raw by it; and they saw in it, beyond their taut day-to-day, meal-to-meal existence, all its hideous potential for the future. All this was hidden behind the flat face of those drab communiqués which security and war impose on us. Behind the words "flying bombs were again launched against southern England; damage and casualties have been reported", there lay, and indeed still lie, a million unrecorded thoughts, not so much about what the doodlebug did to the world of England in 1944 as the world of the future it foreshadowed for us all.

If the country citizen in Kent and Sussex lived through the summer in a state of tautness and grim anger, justified by his own phlegmatic English courage, he knew that he had always, wherever he was, two chances. They were terribly simple. The flying bomb would either fall or fly on. Since in plain fact the bomb was not meant for him, his second chance was good. In London the citizen had only one chance. He knew that the bomb must fall there. He knew quite well that it was intended for him. The target was not the matchless countryside of Kent and Sussex, but the vast and congested area of London.

"They lived through the summer of 1944 in a state of tautness and grim anger, justified by courage." This scene of furniture piled up outside homes in The Crescent, Selhurst, near Croydon was taken after a doodlebug landed during the night of July 27-28th.

London was the Bull's Eye, but Dover was the hottest place in "Hell's Corner" and here the flying bomb campaign brought a new dimension of fear to Kent's most-bombed town. As the doodlebugs were rattling overhead, the series of tunnels which ran under the White Cliffs became a permanent home for hundreds of children.

CHAPTER SIX

The Bull's Eye was everywhere

IN Scotland Yard, the modest red and white building of Whitehall, mythically represented by hundreds of detective writers and gravely viewed every day by thousands of American soldier sightseers, there hangs a map of the Metropolitan Police area of London. It represents the largest urban-human target in the world. Twenty miles across, covering two cities and 94 boroughs, living space for eight million people, home of historic monuments and churches and every kind of building from the Dickensian slums of the east to the garden suburbs of the north-west and the palaces of Kings; huge, congested, monstrous, unmistakable, a target that cannot be missed.

Its very enormity allows the greatest margin of inaccuracy. If you aim at the docks and hit the Guildhall, if you aim at Victoria Station and hit the Tower of London, if you aim at Battersea Power Station and hit the house where Dickens wrote Pickwick Papers, it does not really matter. You are always very near the bull's eye! You never miss. The impossible immensity of London together with its geographical position in relation to the Continent creates for it dangers unknown in the same degree by any other city in the world. To the aimers of the flying bombs, London was the perfect target. They knew that an error of as much as twenty miles still gave them a score.

It was, therefore, very natural that on the afternoon of August 3rd Mr Churchill, giving to a crowded House of Commons a report of the first seven weeks of fly-bomb war, should have spoken at once of "famous and mighty London". He knew quite well that London is not only the greatest material target but the greatest propaganda target in the world. He knew also, as the following words show, that the Germans placed that propaganda value first and its material value second.

"If the Germans imagine that the continuance of this present attack, which has cost them very dear in every branch of production, will have the slightest effect upon the course of the war or upon the resolve of the nation or upon the morale of the men, women and children under

fire they will only be making another of those psychological blunders
for which they have so long been celebrated . . .There is no question
of diverting our strength from the extreme prosecution of the war, or
of allowing this particular infliction to weaken in any way our
energetic support of our Allies."

Nevertheless, Mr Churchill knew and now quite frankly stated, that
the material cost of those first seven weeks was very great. He had the
painful job of announcing, in figures that were a shock to the rest of
England and the outside world, exactly what had been happening to
what had been known as "southern England."

In seven weeks, 5,340 flying bombs had been launched, or more
than 100 per day; 4,735 persons had been killed, with 14,000 more or
less seriously injured. There had been many slightly injured. It was
"a tale of human sorrow and suffering". Yet looked at in the least
distressing way, it meant that each bomb launched had killed on an
average one person. If the bomb was not so costly in life as had been
feared, it was very costly in property. It was terrifying in its surface
blast. In six weeks it had totally destroyed 17,000 houses and had
damaged 800,000 more. By blasting windows and roofs over a
tremendous area it had made thousands homeless. It had split families,
disorganised social life; had driven out of London about 1,000,000
people who had no war business there.

At the same time, with that curious disregard for danger which is part
of the inexplicable essence of living, about the same number of people
appeared to be coming back to London as were leaving it. Foolhardy
though it might have been, as Mr Churchill pointed out, that fact gave
"the lie in most effective measure to the fantastic German stories of
London being in panic under the perpetual pall of smoke and flame".

Nevertheless fly-bomb horrors were very many and very real; and
Mr Churchill could offer no hope that they would end. On that day,
August 3rd, the Allied line in Normandy ran from Avranches to Caen;
the greater part of the flying bomb bases were a hundred miles to the
east. Until they were captured the flying bomb menace could not end.
Nor, in all probability, would it end then. It was known that flying
bombs could be launched from carrier aircraft and it was known also
that the flying bomb, which the Germans liked to call V1, was likely
sooner or later to be replaced or supplemented by V2. That weapon,

Mr Churchill, in his statement to the House of Commons, described the flying bomb campaign as a tale of human sorrow and suffering with 4,735 people killed and more than 14,000 seriously injured. He could offer no hope that the bombing would soon end. One of the worst incidents, which the Prime Minister did not specifically mention, occurred at lunchtime on June 30th. High above the Strand, the engine of a missile cut out and it glided down silently, striking the road 40 feet in front of the Air Ministry building in the Aldwych. A peaceful summer scene was turned into one of dreadful carnage with 48 killed. The photographs which were taken shortly after the incident show two of the injured — a delivery man and a city worker.

of which Mr Churchill had warned the House in February, would in all probability be a stratospheric rocket of greater range, greater power and even greater inaccuracy than the first. It might even be followed by another, V3 and even, if you were to believe the propaganda threats by Dr Goebbels, by V4. Whatever these weapons were and however they might come, they were intended, as Mr Churchill said, "to produce a great deal more mischief".

The Churchillian statement of that afternoon was necessarily general and incomplete. It could only hint at the vast organisations behind the scenes; the long prepared plans for Civil Defence, National Fire Service, Health Services, Police Services, hospitals, railways, buses, shelters, feeding centres, evacuation; building repairs, emergency housing and the care of young and aged and sick. It could only hint at the state of morale and whether, if it was high or low, it had changed since the blitz of 1940. It could only touch on the broad grey lines and not the thin bitter personal etchings of trial and suffering. It could say nothing of the sharp humour, the dry resignation, the incongruous comedies of the first seven weeks of the new menace to civilised living.

In point of fact much had been done. Much had changed. All the vast organisations which are the foundation of morale in times of crisis — hospitals, Civil Defence, fire services and so on — had changed their methods as their experience grew. All of them had been warned of the possible coming of the flying bomb; all of them had made arrangements to meet it. Yet none of them knew what the flying bomb would do when it came and, most of all, what it would do to morale. In reality it did a great deal to morale. Its effects were in some ways violently different from the effect of the blitz of 1940. In that year the bomb had driven people closer together; it had drawn them closer into communities for shelter, feeding, clothing, friendliness and comfort. In 1944 the flying bomb seemed to drive them apart. In 1940 there were few personal shelters; a vast population slept in the Tubes. In 1944 tens of thousands of houses in London had their personal shelters, some of Anderson type outside or Morrison type inside, others of the reinforced basement type under the house. There were also great numbers of street shelters. To all these, which were part of the street or the house, the people tended to cling with that peculiar tenacity of

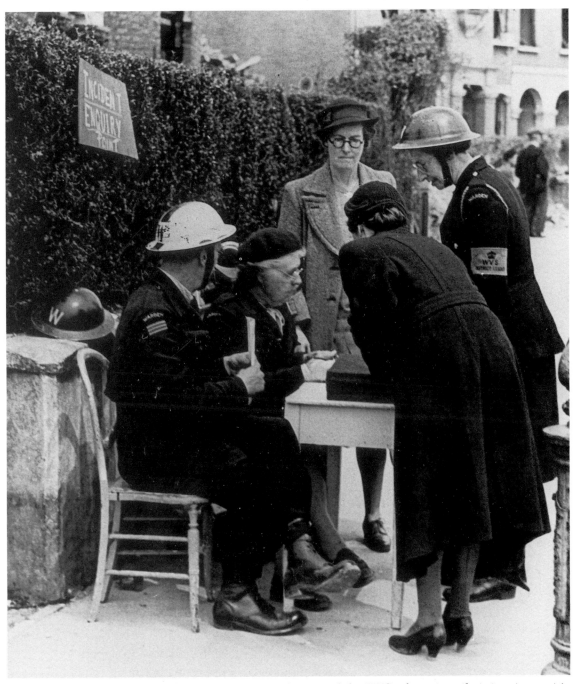

"More mischief" meant more work for the Civil Defence and the WVS who set up their inquiry post in Woodville Road, Croydon, following a "flying bomb incident" during the night of July 4th-5th, 1944. Throughout the campaign, the Women's Voluntary Service worked alongside the ARP wardens, firemen and all those in the front line of rescue work. They cooked, they washed up, they gave comfort, they acted as nurses, messengers and escorts — and they set up their inquiry points every time a doodlebug landed.

pride and affection which makes the Englishman's home his castle.

No longer, in fact, did the citizen tend to leave his home when the bomb menaced it or the bomb fell. He clung to it instead. That admirable organisation, the Women's Voluntary Service, noted in the course of its tireless and wonderful work all over the bombed areas that it was no longer easy to bring bombed citizens to feeding centres. Food had to be taken to the people. Kerbside feeding replaced communal feeding. More and more people refused to leave their bombed homes. They worked frantically in the chaos. The police of the much-bombed district of Croydon noted the same thing. Women were found dusting with scrupulous care the window sills of blasted houses, excusing themselves with "Must make it look a bit decent, you know" — expressing that pride of street and house which is more than self-respect. This same intense desire to hold on to normal life was seen also in the crazy behaviour of a young man who insisted, against all threats and advice, on going back into a house that was about to collapse. "Knock 'im down, guv'nor, I can't do nuthin' with 'im", said his father to the policeman, "Knock 'im down afore he does 'isself any 'arm." The young man grew very excited. "You see, guv'nor, I'm being married this morning and all me money's in the 'ouse and I gotta get it somehow." So the policeman gave permission for the boy to go into the house: at which there was no longer any controlling his father. "Blimey, guv'nor, if he's goin' in I'm goin' in! I gotta pair o' boots in there."

To this category also belongs the old lady with the black leather bag. She is a spiritual sister to the old lady who said "They ain't human", and to the other old lady who said "Ain't they sly?". She is the one with the thousand ladies all over London who have been carrying their black bags to the shelters every night for five years and whose constant watchword has been "Damn Hitler. Where's my Guiness?" As this old lady crawled out from under the debris of her smashed house, shaken, covered with dust, bruised, she thought only of her black leather bag. "Is me bag all right?" she said. "Yes", they said, the bag was alright. Was there something important in it? "I'll say it's important", she said, "it's me bottle of whisky." In that case, they suggested, this was probably a good time for her to take a drop. "Not on your life", the old lady said. "I'm saving that for an emergency."

The Women's Voluntary Service provided garments for people who had lost everything but the things they stood up in and they delivered hot midday meals to hundreds of schools in doodlebug alley. Above, Paddington. Below, Surrey.

The woman dusting the window-ledge where there is no longer any window, the young man fighting to rescue his marriage money, the old ladies clinging, through their symbolic black bags, to a life that even in its extremes of terror never becomes a 'time of emergency': all these are part of the story of London morale. But they are not the whole story. Morale is not compounded of tangible experience. It is something in the air.

And the something that was in the London air of summer 1944 was very different from the something that was in the air in winter 1940. Morale had not fallen; it had simply grown thinner. People were distracted and bewildered rather than very afraid. When courage has to be spread over twenty-four hours of the days it grows thin towards the end of them. The Londoner has always shown a singular tenacity about his city. Now both the WVS and the Police noted that this tenacity had become more personal. Londoners began to cling to their own bits of London, shattered or whole, and something pathetic and wonderful was to be seen in their bewildered devotion to shapeless scraps of what had once been home. The scraps were sometimes not even shapeless. The doodlebug in the space of a clouded split second blew the mansion, the hospital, the cottage, the top floor back room into a tower of dark dust that settled into something indistinguishable from the dust of a Nineveh and Pompeii. The bomb-ruin is not only international but timeless too.

The WVS, tireless, superbly efficient, infinitely adaptable, fed this thinned morale from mobile canteens, cars, even hand-carts. It distributed hot meals, tea, chewing gum from America, gallons of chocolate. It helped to evacuate from the city 307,768 mothers, in 500 special trains. It sent 3,000 of its members with them; and with the members 7,000 urns of tea. In one week of July it evacuated 1,448 expectant mothers. It provided 200,000 garments for people who had lost everything but the things they stood up in. It provided in one day 576 babies' bottles and 1,152 teats. It evacuated children under five and, most difficult of all, people of over 65. Its organisation, in which the la-di-da milady worked side by side with the cockney street warden, was everywhere, at all times, night and day, wherever bombs were coming down. They earned for themselves that rarest of all tributes: the tribute given by the North to the South. It came from a Lancashire man sent to London on bomb-damage reconstruction. He

The WVS on the march. From all parts of the country they came to cook and wash up for the 3,000 builders who volunteered to patch up London during the flying bomb campaign. The WVS also helped with the Re-homing Scheme and gave more than material help towards the reconstruction of many shattered homes.

had never seen or heard a bomb in his life; he was a man to whom, as to thousands of others, a siren sounding an alert was a fearful event and who, as the flying bombs began to fall, promptly took up his bed and dived into the nearest and deepest shelter. He was arrested in his flight by the sight of WVS drivers, not all of them young, but all of them certainly tired, calmly going out on duty into a concentration of doodlebugs. His courage came back. Next day he was heard to say, in a classic sentence which it is to be hoped the censor will tolerate since those of whom it was made are very proud of it: "See them? Them's best bloody bitches in t'world."

Figures tell something, but not all. The Lancashire man with his crisp and coloured tribute says more for an army of women than all its own impressive figures of work and succour can ever do. So with the damaged home. Figures will tell you that a single fly bomb causes damage within an area of 20 or 30 acres, demolishes beyond repair 20 or 30 houses, slightly damages 400 — 1,000 others. Yet the picture of an old lady on the train going north, holding the canary in its cage in one hand and her grandson in the other, and in her glassy, flabby eyes a look of "So this, after all, is what we have come to", tells of something that is too deep for tears. In the same way the miles and miles of anonymous blasted roofs all across south and south east London meet the eye and only succeed, after a time, in tiring it. The real picture only comes alive at the sight of thousands and thousands of hay-rick tarpaulins, bright green and grey and brown, sent from farmers and builders all over the country, spread over the tileless roofs of the city.

DIY, born a few years earlier in the Blitz, continued during the summer and autumn of 1944, housewives generally making their own temporary repairs to blasted windows.

"Miles and miles of anonymous blasted roofs meet the eye." This panoramic picture of bomb damage in Navarre Road, East Ham was taken by Ted Carter, Chief ARP Warden for Waltham Holy Cross on February 2nd, 1945. The damage was caused by a rocket which completely cleared three sides of a square block of homes. Miraculously, considering the extent of the blast, there were only two slight casualties.

"More blasted roofs." This was Queen Elizabeth Walk, Addington shattered by a doodlebug on the night of June 28th-29th, 1944

The flying bomb which struck the Guards Chapel in Wellington Barracks on June 18th, 1944 could not have arrived at a more unfortunate time — in the middle of a special service for both active and retired guardsmen and their guests. The bomb hit the roof, which had been reinforced during the Blitz to withstand incendiary bombs, and crashed into the Chapel before its warhead went off. The blast blew the roof away and pulverised the side walls and supporting pillars. 121 people were killed and 141 injured. Only the Bishop of Maidstone was unhurt; he had been conducting the service and was saved by the dome over the altar. One survivor told of a loud buzzing that turned into a high pitched whine followed by the explosion. After that everything went quiet until he heard a woman's voice singing in the darkness 'The Rose of Tralee'.

CHAPTER SEVEN
Good blokes, those firemen!

THE heap of rubble that was a London home never had any meaning for us, the outside world. But the heap of rubble that was the Guards' Chapel at Buckingham Gate in London meant something to us all. On a fine Sunday summer morning, as the roses were coming into bloom beyond the plane trees in the park across the road, a whole congregation of serving soldiers, men and women, were lost with the chapel in which they worshipped. From that time onward, an average of one historic building of one sort or another was damaged or destroyed in London every day. The lovely Staple Inn, Holborn, St George's Church in Westminster Street, Holland House in Kensington, the Palace in Fulham, the Friends' Meeting House in Hammersmith, the Customs House and five churches in the City of London, Charlton House in Greenwich, Dulwich College in Camberwell, the Cathedral in Southwark — day after day London added another name to its already long list of damaged historic treasure.

The fly bomb, as we have seen, could never miss. It fell in the gardens of the poor and in the gardens of Buckingham Palace. And it fell mostly south of the Thames, in those tightly congested boroughs that were the nineteenth century's contribution to town planning. Into these miles and miles of streets, from the mean desolation of the riverside wharf alleys made more desolate by the bombing of 1940, to the lighter outer suburbias of Croydon and Penge, the fly bombs poured in on their fixed routes with shocking reiteration. The theory that no two bombs ever fall in the same place was disproved again and again. Robot design and robot power made it certain that they would often do so. Flying in from the south east they made landfall time after time just short of the city's centre. The boroughs of Croydon, Penge, Beckenham, Dulwich, Streatham and Lewisham were under the severest sort of bombardment day after day. The little Victorian borough of Penge, tiny beside the huge area of neighbouring Croydon, claims to have suffered more, for its size, than any other area in London.

Penge at least will show what can happen to a single congested area. Penge is a mile square, its post-Victorian facade has a look of substance since proved to be false. It has 6,000 houses. Yet in 80 days it had 10,000 houses damaged. This odd statement is explicable by the fact that some thousands of houses were damaged a second time. And after evacuation one in 20 of the remaining population was killed or injured. The rest had, literally, no roof over their heads.

Let Penge then, with a few general figures, finish off the picture of all the south and south-eastern area of metropolitan London as it looked by the middle of August. And let the builders — whose job in this blitz made the job of practically any other service look by comparison quite small— supply the figures. By the end of July production of window-covering materials had increased to a million yards a week. Each week two million tiles and two million slates were brought to London. Of those picturesque hayrick covers already mentioned there were 150,000 in use, together with unnumbered thousands of ladders, at one time. And in addition, there arrived or were calculated as being necessary in the long future of reconstruction:

> *150 million tiles or slates*
> *200 million square feet of ceiling and wallboard*
> *50 million square feet of glass*
> *400 thousand doors*
> *40 thousand lavatory basins*
> *50 thousand sinks*
> *50 thousand WC cisterns*
> *70 thousand WC pans*
> *50 thousand water storage tanks*

To all these demands for the very fundamental necessities of human living were added demands for furniture, crockery, bedding — all the things, officially known as goods and chattels, that make up home. Much furniture was salvageable. This in itself created a big problem of removal and storage. Let Croydon and Wandsworth supply the figures this time. In Wandsworth, 125 bombs made necessary no less than 7,000 removals, of which 4,200 went to store. In Croydon 142, bombs made 3,000 removals necessary, of which exactly half went to store. All this was repeated in twenty other boroughs. Soldiers, RAF, American forces, rescue workers and contractors all helped, in fact, to

Whitehall Road, Thornton Heath received its flying bomb on June 30th, 1944

Croydon was the most fly-bombed borough in London. Between Thursday June 15th, 1944 and the end of the terror in 1945, 142 doodlebugs crashed in Croydon, killing 211 people and injuring more than 2,000. Almost 59,000 houses were damaged and of these 1,400 were completely destroyed. As in all the boroughs of London a great body of men, both civilian and Service, were drafted in to repair and make safe, damaged property. By June, over 24,000 homes were being damaged every 24 hours and the backlog was increasing by 12,000 a day. From all over the country came the volunteer workers. They gathered at special assembly points for the allocation of food and accommodation. The photograph was taken in Pembury Road, South Norwood, near Croydon on July 5th, 1944, following yet another "flying bomb incident".

salvage enough furniture for no less than 50,000 removals.

In all this work and terror and desolation and disruption there was, happily, little fire. The flying bomb did its work by blast; not by incendiaries. In 1940 and again in the early months of 1944 it had been quite different. Fire was the great enemy.   In these early days of the war there was no such thing as a National Fire Service. Fire brigades were inclined to be parochial. They had no unity except among themselves; they worked within the restricted area of their own locality; they had different uniforms and different rates of pay. The idea of the fireman of Canterbury being sent to help with a fire in London, would have been quite revolutionary. But war and incendiaries made high mobility not only necessary but imperative. With the war, in fact, firemen became nationalised. They had national uniform, national rates of pay, national obligations and a national name.

All this meant that their direction could be centralised. At its headquarters on the banks of the Thames, the NFS can see, on the board of its magnificent operations room, the immediate available strength of its pumps and tenders all over London. By radio it can move and marshal them like the commander of an air force or an army. It controls millions of gallons of water at a touch. In the blitzes of 1940 and 1941, in the days when the bitterest lessons about fire had to be learned within the fire, the firemen of London once laid a length of hose nine miles long. It faced great difficulties when the enemy bombed the city at low tide by the river, from which much fire-fighting water came. It suffered greatly because of bombed water mains. By 1944 it had learned its lessons from all these things. It had made available to itself millions of gallons of static and emergency water, thousands of pumps. It could direct and redirect its men to the scenes of great fires exactly as a general moves his reserves to the scenes of attack.

The NFS was, therefore, more than ready for what the flying bomb might do. It was probably, by the spring of 1944, the most intensively organised and experienced fire-service in the world. It had learnt much and was ready for more. But when the first flying-bombs began to fall in London in the middle of June it became obvious that many problems of the past were not to be renewed. In surface effect the bomb was terrific; in subterranean effect it was very slight. It was too shallow to reach either gas mains or water mains. Moreover, it rarely created

Thousands of volunteers from the north and west country came to patch up houses in London and southern England. The work was punishing — often 12 hours a day, seven days a week — for it was a race against time to make houses weatherproof before winter set in. The first stage was a temporary tarpaulin and the second was the actual repair of roofs. In September, the Minister for Reconstruction revealed that 21,000 men and 7,000 Servicemen were at work repairing 1.1 million damaged homes. The two men above are dragging the tarpaulin over the roof of a house at Onslow Square, Belgravia to keep out the July rain.

serious fire, except on such occasions as when it dropped on factories storing great quantities of oil or on bus depots of London Transport.

Out of 2,299 incidents in the London area there were, however, 933 fires: small fires begun by broken gas pipes; spectacular fires like the great riverside burning of a candle factory; difficult fires like the distillation plant where burning tar ran like black lava down the streets; fires at paint works, gas works, fuel research works, garages. All these fires were widely distributed. The concentrated firing of a city, as in December 1940, never again became a possibility.

Firemen are, however, not only firemen. It has been very well said of London wartime firemen that in learning to be firemen they have also learned to be citizens. In learning to be citizens they have also learned to be rescue workers, first aid workers, salvagers of furniture and home. Twenty nine thousand of them, whole time men and women with 26,000 part timers, were more than necessary for dealing with the fires of the doodlebug. Out of this force of 55,000 people the NFS created a citizen service that rescued trapped fly bomb victims, cleared debris for ambulances and stretcher bearers, salvaged furniture, calmed the fears of those who waited in those curious and awful silences when rescue parties listen for the voices that faintly call from under the shambles of home. Men in the battlefield of Normandy, fed by doodlebug propaganda from the enemy, got letters from their wives that were a counterblast — "We got all the furniture out, or nearly all. The firemen risked their lives"— and reassured, wrote back "Good to know we got such good blokes back home".

Good blokes — that odd understated description is practically the highest praise the Englishman can give. Good blokes — mucking in, building a tunnel under a mountain of bricks as carefully for a trapped dog as for a woman or child, turning doors into stretchers, turning the difficult night into easy night by the use of their powerful arc lights so that rescue work could go on, putting in 18,000 hours on ARP work, tens of thousands of man days on jobs not really their own. Good blokes — good work; brave, wretched, sad and decent unromantic work. "The fireman's experience is not to be found," wrote one fireman of distinction, "in the pretty orange frontispiece surmounted by a romantic bundle of nightdress waiting for its succour."

All of this work had death in it: dust and death. Even the live victims

For the children of "flying bomb alley", the WVS clothing depots were in constant use. Here brother and sister Anne and Michael have been brought to a centre by their mother while, on the right, Sheila tries on a longer skirt. The WVS teams at the clothing depots were kept particularly busy dealing with evacuees who did not possess adequate wardrobes while other sections of the WVS often had to trace the lost luggage of those who did.

of the doodlebug came out of their bomb traps wearing a grey dusty mask of desolation and always after the fall of the bomb there was the high tower of dark smoke dust and then, in the summer air, the dead sick stench of high explosive strong as corruption and sour as tombs. It is hard to live in such air, harder still to work. How many romantic boyhood fire-fighting ambitions are buried under the dust of London with the broken limbs of children and the disintegrated life of centuries? Ask a fireman — "There are things that nauseate me in this business of fire-fighting. The smell of burning and disintegration ... constant ... solid".

Behind that romantic clanging of bells there simply lay, for London's firemen, weeks and weeks of slogging work that had in it, day after day, a terrible monotony. Everywhere that work was finely and decently done.

Sharing it were the Civil Defence services of London. They were responsible for roughly the same area as that of the Metropolitan Police, the same unmissable target of 724 square miles. They controlled the whole of the administrative County of London, the county of Middlesex, certain parts of Hertfordshire, large borough areas of Essex, Surrey and Kent. They controlled altogether 94 boroughs, more than 17,000 full time women and men.

Like the NFS, with whom they worked always in admirable combination, they had made considerably careful preparations for the defence of London in the event of the enemy's retaliation on or before the invasion of the Continent began. Fortunately the enemy was in no position to attack us, or decided that it would not be advantageous to attack us, either with piloted aircraft or with flying bombs, until after invasion had started. The fact that no attempt was made to interrupt the vast preparations in the docks of London was an amazing thing. But all the preparations were made against such an attempt and they are worth briefly describing.

Special fire patrols were posted on every ship in London's dock while it was being loaded with petrol, ammunition or general stores. Every ship was linked by telephone to the nearest NFS station. Hose was laid out, suctions were ready, fire boats stationed alongside all the larger ships, foam was provided on jetties, foam engines stationed. Every ship, both in the dock and at waiting berths, was checked and

More flying bombs have fallen in London overnight, dislocating the water supply to scores of homes. Help for the housewives is not far away. The National Emergency Washing Service van is called to the area where washing is marked and sorted by the supervisor. The individual bundles then go into the van where the trained staff wash, dry and iron. No charge is made — it's all part of the service in "doodlebugged" London.

registered. As a result seventeen minor fires were never allowed to reach a point where they could do any serious damage to those ships.

All this, and especially the fact that the enemy did not attempt any sort of interference with the preparations at the port, greatly relieved the anxieties of Civil Defence. When flying bombs eventually began to fall it was able to concentrate all its energies on dealing with them and it was able to see, with relief, that many of the problems of 1940 and 1941 would not recur. Like the NFS, it found the effect of the bomb rather like that of a parachute mine. Its penetrative power was small except when it fell with the engine running. There were few broken gas mains and water mains. Night casualties were light. Day casualties on the whole were heavier because of crowded buildings and streets. A breakfast-time bomb on a block of flats at Sloane Court killed 74, a lunchtime bomb in crowded Aldwych killed 46. In Lewisham's busy shopping street a bomb gliding silently down on to the market place killed 59 in a crowded store.

These general figures conceal rather than reveal the real tasks of Civil Defence. A flying bomb that falls in a field makes a mark like a shallow brown saucer. A flying bomb falling on a high building brings down tons of masonry. It pins its victims, dead or alive, into a dangerous and colossal trap. This trap has somehow to be broken open, not crudely, as a man with a battering ram runs at a wall, but delicately and patiently and intelligently, rather as a burglar breaks open a safe by the touch of his fingers on the lock. To discover which way joists run, if basement walls are sound, what are the size and extent of rooms and passages — all this will affect the technique of tunnelling under debris. This tunnelling is at all times dangerous and delicate. Haste and clumsiness will bring down a mountain of ruin, burying and killing rescuers and victims alike.

Take two examples of this:

(a) A three storey building and cellar has collapsed on itself. It leaves two flank walls, sixty tons weight together, ready to collapse. The street wall is fifteen inches out of plumb; only a tie rod keeps it from falling. Neither debris nor walls can be disturbed. Only careful and patient tunnelling can reach six casualties, of which two are rescued alive, one after an arm had been amputated by a rescue worker under the supervision of a doctor giving anaesthetic.

This was south London's worst flying bomb incident of all. At 9.41 am on the morning of Friday July 18th, a V1 exploded in front of the clock tower in Lewisham High Street catching shoppers completely unawares. The market stalls in a line outside Marks and Spencer's, Woolworths and Sainsbury's caught the full force of the blast. So did two passing buses which were blown to pieces and the nearby post office which was full of old age pensioners. The bomb actually exploded on the roof of the shelter demolishing shops on both sides of the road. Firemen, ambulances and volunteers arrived quickly and were greeted by an appalling carnage for 59 people were killed and more than 300 injured. The WVS set up their inquiry point in less than ten minutes and immediately ordered mobile meal canteens, baths and laundries.

(b) A lodging house for 250 is lifted bodily upward and then collapses on itself. After the explosion, floors remain whole in compressed sandwich form, separated by depth of cross joints. From pockets formed by smashed cubicles casualties were rescued mainly alive. Bulldozers and cranes worked night and day, lifting debris straight from building to truck, until it was certain no casualty remained.

This sort of incident , with thousands of them that varied in size and problems involved, occurred all across London. Yet in tackling them the Mobile Civil Defences were never stretched on operational work. The help of the NFS, Home Guard and British and American soldiers was great; much help was also received from other Allied soldiers. The post-raid services and wardens, on whom the real strain fell, were at all times prodigious in their energy and devotion. It is impossible to give even a list of their deeds. Out of all the scores of types that make up their great numbers it is enough, perhaps, to mention one. Everywhere there was praise for the older man: particularly, and indeed most of all, for that great London type, the old sweat. Slow, grey, solid, inexorable, taciturn, tireless, he slogged on through countless tons of London ruin, beating younger men in stamina, craft and the desire to do the job for the job's sake only. Odd that he was so often the man who, forty years ago, had helped with trowel and muck and brick and plaster to build much of suburban London up. Odd that he should now, in middle age, be the man with pick and shovel and basket and crowbar to help knock so much of it down.

The plaster he had slapped on in what was really another world now covered him with dust. This dust was one of the protagonists of the doodlebug drama. It covered everything within a large radius of the bomb-fall. It covered streets and roofs and trees. It covered casualties, so that on many occasions the casualty rate appeared at first sight to be appallingly high, for the blown dust covered its victims with a ghastly grey bloom that was like the mask of death. Again and again this dust was washed off by trained nurses, of whom there were 430 in London Region, or auxiliaries, of whom there were nearly 13,000 — to reveal underneath only the slightest injuries. From hospital most of such cases went home in two days.

The other protagonist in the drama was glass. It was more dangerous

Audrey Russell, one of the pioneering voices of BBC news reporting, is seen here on one of her "vintage" outside broadcast assignments for Radio Newsreel — a long-running programme which began in 1940. Audrey is talking to Mrs Cunningham whose home "somewhere in southern England" has been destroyed by a flying bomb. Audrey Russell is remembered for her ability to provide well-constructed and beautifully modulated sentences, known at the time as "word pictures".

and more deadly than dust. Driven everywhere, in myriad splinters, by the force of explosions, it caused more injuries than anything else. People in shopping streets were caught in a bright hell of flying slivers hideously dangerous to eyes and face and hands. Glass pock-marked its lesser victims with tiny bloody scars that stood out brightly on the shocked white flesh. It gashed its worst victims with slashes like those of a broad sword. It buried itself into the flesh as it buried itself into the polished surfaces of furniture, the fruit of glasshouses, the food of grocers' shops. The sharp, dreary sound of it being swept up on dry summer pavements was a dead and pointless sound. It seemed to symbolise, far more than the great piles of dusty ruins, the wretchedness of war that attacks the citizen and the home.

The citizen's instinctive defence against blast and glass was to drop flat on his face and then cover it with his hands. But there were some who could not do this; the aged and, of course, the smallest of children. It became very rapidly obvious that London was no place for any of them to be. So a kind of war that no longer made its attack on soldiers armed to meet it began to drive the future citizens of London out of the city. They went, in thousands. For the tiniest of them, those under five, no less than 13,000 cots were ready in the country, contained altogether in about 400 nurseries; for those tiniest of children, some of whom are motherless, could not be billeted in strange homes on strange people by compulsory power. Even where they had mothers it was not always possible for the mother, because of work or injury, to go with them. For the evacuation of such mites there were no fewer than 60,000 applications, in itself an appalling commentary on the direction of modern war. Yet even before many of them could be got away — still more appalling fact — 22 babies were killed in one London nursery, another public assistance nursery was totally wrecked, and another receiving centre was bombed. Perhaps this is the place also to point out that in the entire London area no less than 151 hospitals were hit, some of them repeatedly, 41 of them seriously.

The official evacuation scheme for London was opened — more correctly perhaps reopened — on Saturday July 5th, about three weeks after the first bombs had begun to fall. Numbers of people, both grown up and children, had of course already left by their own resources. The official scheme was voluntary. It provided, as we have seen, for the

The winners and the losers in a cruel game of fate. Above are the remains of St John's School, Shirley, near Croydon, blasted by a doodlebug on July 26, 1944. No-one was hurt. The teachers heard the alert and the children trooped obediently to the safety of the air-raid shelter.

There was no such happy ending at Crockham Hill, near Westerham in Kent, where an isolated building used as a nursery for evacuated London children, was struck by a V1 in the early hours of Friday June 30th, 1944. The house collapsed upon the sleeping infants leaving only a chimney stack and the shell of the gardener's cottage still standing. Twenty two of the 30 children, all aged under five, were killed. Many of them had just been sent there for safety. Eight out of the 11 nurses and domestic staff also died and all the other occupants were seriously injured. The incident occurred less than a mile from Winston Churchill's country home at Chartwell.

mites under five, school children from five to 16; mothers with children under five; other people who wished to go. Bus loads of waving children, all labelled like parcels, all singing popular songs, all very very noisy, rode to the North and West London stations and made for a few days what little gaiety there was in this depressing necessity. School teachers went with them. And they went in that excited atmosphere made rather more crazy by sickness, fainting, accident and all the awkward bodily needs of children in mass, and they went in special trains of which only the drivers, firemen and guards knew the destination. Two thousand four hundred of them arrived in Blackpool on Monday the 7th, by which time 16,500 had already left London. Others went to Shropshire, the Midlands, Lancashire, Scotland, the West.

Impressions? The child's reaction to war is curious. In 1940 the evacuated children of London cried for mum and dad; cried for home; cried for fear of the unknown in the country. In 1944 they knew the ropes; some of them had no home; they knew what the country was like. And mum and dad? "My dad's in Italy." "My mum's in munitions." "I ain't got no Dad. He was killed in Africa." Small wonder that an American Sergeant, watching them as they went, said "Gee, this brings tears to my eyes. Wait'll I get at the damned Fritzes again". His, perhaps, were not the only grown-up tears; but the tears of children were, on the whole, very few. In a few hours they found themselves in that world to which the London child's reaction in 1940 became a legend. "Cor blimey don't your taters grow in boxes? Cor, they get the milk out of cows instead of bottles!" Now the reaction was different. They were quick to note that the Midlands, the North and Scotland were part of a world long since comfortably remote from war. "Don't you get no sirens here?" expresses completely all their wonder.

By August 3rd, when Mr Churchill spoke in the Commons, 225,000 mothers and children had gone into the safety of a world that did not know the sound of the doodlebug. Nearly 1,000,000 people had left London altogether; 17,000 houses had been destroyed in the city they left, 800,000 damaged; 95,000 people, homeless or temporarily homeless, had passed through the official rest centres. Scores of special trains were run by the L.M.S.,L.N.E. and G.W. Railways, to

In early July, 1944, following public demand, the Government opened London's deep shelters which had not been ready for the 1940-41 blitz. More than 4,000 spent a happier night underground.

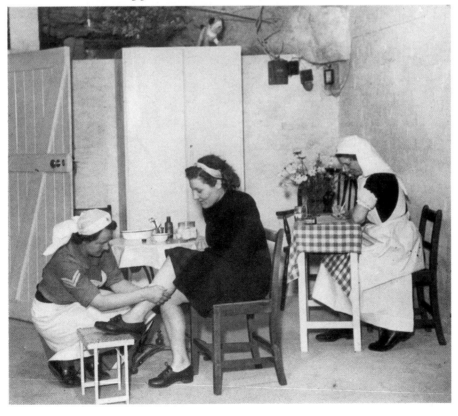

Thousands of children from south London were evacuated — but not all of them. Many made their homes in the network of caves at Chislehurst; in fact at one time more than 15,000 people lived in this small town below ground. The Cave Committee ran the operation with clockwork efficiency. There was a cinema, church, telephone kiosk, savings bank, first aid post and shops.

whom the largest possible tribute is due. All these and indeed all normal trains out of London were crowded. Yet everyone, including Mr Churchill, noted a curious thing. The trains coming into London were just as crowded as those going out. In that incongruous fact there was a touch of defiance and stoicism that was quietly flung by the people of Britain into the face of the future. It was the answer to the worst the bomb could bring. Add to this one other fact, and you have a picture of war that defies analysis. The clothes provided for the bombed-out babies of 1940 were too small for the bombed-out babies of 1944. These babies, born after five years of war and in a time of bloodshed and anxiety, were fatter, heavier and healthier than the babies of better days.

As doodlebugs and later rockets continued to pound London and the south-east, there was a rapid increase in the number of people sheltering in the Underground. By the end of July more than 70,000 were sleeping on station platforms and many remained underground all day. There were other safe locations including the tunnels which linked the chalk pits at Northfleet in Kent (above).

This dramatic photograph shows a flying bomb actually taking off from a village site in northern France. Even today, 50 years on, there are Frenchmen who can graphically recall the terrifying spectacle of a V1 take-off which was like 100 bombs going off at the same time. Windows in the houses and cottages for miles around would rattle and others would be blown into a thousand fragments by the concussion. One villager recalled: "I remember the sky and surrounding countryside being lit up with a blinding flash of fiery red light and an object like a meteor racing across the heavens with the roar of an express train". Sometimes, like a mad dog, the doodlebug would turn on its masters and crash near those who had set it on its crazy course.

CHAPTER EIGHT

La Casserole. It bubbled as it flew!

VISITORS to Northern France in the days after the war will probably find themselves besieged by gentlemen anxious to take them on tours of the battlefields. Equally, in any village from Caen to Calais, they will find unlimited numbers of Frenchmen, French women and especially French children prepared to give them all the information they need about the German secret weapon of 1944: *la bomb volante*, called by some Frenchmen *la casserole* because it bubbled like a monstrous stew-pot as it flew, and known all over France, as it was probably known over Europe, as V1 — English pronunciation.

The countryside of northern France from Normandy to the Pas de Calais has in it much that reminds the Englishman of home. The colour and shape of the land is very like that of Kent, Sussex and Hampshire: woodland and pasture, low hills and orchards, farmstead and gardens, white cliffs and cathedral towns. The villages are more primitive, more dusty, more muddy, more simple and more remote than the villages of England. They are nearer to the villages of Ireland; the big stone farm houses, beside which the cider apples are poured in russet and golden piles in September, might have come out of stories of Maupassant; the huge crumbling chateaux are part of the 18th century.

Twice within five years this countryside has proved itself indefensible in war. Yet from the air it looks like a dense and intricate mass of roads and woodland, in which an army could lie low and hidden and defy the worst. This, in fact, is what the Germans did. They hid here, in the years 1942, 1943 and 1944, an army of soldiers, conscripted workers and enforced labourers whose ultimate weapon was to be the flying bomb. The country was admirably suited to their plan. It was possible to contain within it hundreds and, if necessary, thousands of launching and supply sites, all within a range of about 130 miles of London, practically all of them orientated to that city. All of those sites could be covered by the natural camouflage of the country and, under the protection of woods and lanes and orchards, would be difficult to find from the air.

La Casserole. It bubbled as it flew!

The Germans showed great ingenuity and a complete disregard for the people of France in their plan. Their favourite site for a launching ramp was a small wood of five or ten acres close to a hard road, where trees in both summer and winter gave them perfect cover. In such woodland the Germans built hundreds of sites and supply depots. They also chose more domestic sites. Orchards of apple and pear were favourite places. Nor had they any compunction whatsoever about putting them in the back gardens of French peasants in remote villages. On at least one occasion they built an entire launching site in a village street: a site in which the neighbouring French peasants took particular pleasure, for the good reason that on its first launching operation the flying bomb turned an immediate somersault, fell back in the site and killed or buried the entire German crew.

In choosing such sites, many of them surrounded by houses, the Germans were perfectly aware of two things: they knew that they would be well hidden and they knew also that if they were discovered and bombed from the air by British and Allied airforces the French population would suffer greviously. There was, in fact, something diabolical in their seeking protection out of the very fabric of French domestic life, knowing at the same time that that fabric would be smashed to pieces if ever the time came.

The time, as we shall see, did come; but why were the launching sites for a weapon that was, after all, an aeroplane with a fairly large wing-span confined to such small spaces? The answer is that the sites themselves were surprisingly small. After the first 100 ski-sites had been destroyed by bombers of the RAF in the winter of 1943-44, the Germans set about the construction of a much simpler, pre-fabricated site, which could be transported easily to wherever it was needed and assembled there very quickly.

This type, from which the attacks of the summer were launched, was more than anything else like a section of scenic railway. The lines were erected on a base of steel and wooden pillars and, beginning at a few feet above ground level, rose exactly like a railway at a fun fair at an angle of 30 or 35 degrees to the far end. The track, or ramp was about eighty yards long; the narrow railway lines had between them a parallel metal slot like that on a tram track. At a distance of about eight feet outward from each rail ran another rail. The inner track supported

94

The ramp, instead of being supported by massive walls of concrete became a simple, prefabricated, sectionalised set of rails supported on a base of steel and wooden pillars. This one at Belloy-sur-Somme is under construction in a wood — a favourite site for launching La Casserole!

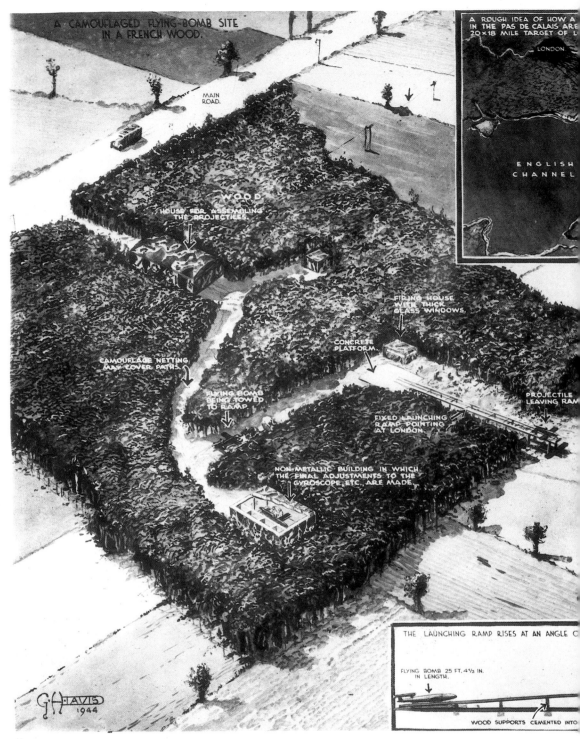

Labels within the drawing:

A CAMOUFLAGED FLYING-BOMB SITE IN A FRENCH WOOD.

A ROUGH IDEA OF HOW A ... IN THE PAS DE CALAIS ARE ... 20×18 MILE TARGET OF L...

LONDON.

ENGLISH CHANNEL

MAIN ROAD.

WOOD

HOUSE FOR ASSEMBLING THE PROJECTILES.

FIRING HOUSE WITH THICK GLASS WINDOWS.

CONCRETE PLATFORM.

CAMOUFLAGE NETTING MAY COVER PATHS.

FLYING BOMB BEING TOWED TO RAMP.

FIXED LAUNCHING RAMP POINTING AT LONDON.

PROJECTILE LEAVING RAM...

NON-METALLIC BUILDING IN WHICH THE FINAL ADJUSTMENTS TO THE GYROSCOPE, ETC., ARE MADE.

THE LAUNCHING RAMP RISES AT AN ANGLE O...

FLYING BOMB 25 FT. 4½ IN. IN LENGTH.

WOOD SUPPORTS CEMENTED INTO...

G.H.DAVIS 1944

This drawing, which appeared in the Illustrated London News of July 15th, 1944, gives a general impression of a flying bomb launching site in a village in northern France. Such sites — and there were several of them — were considerably more simple in design than the original heavily-built concrete installations which had been so heavily bombed by the Allied Airforce.

As the drawing shows, the launching ramps were built at ground level and rose gradually at an angle of approximately seven degrees for a distance of about 200 feet from a concrete platform at the rear to the take-off point at the front of the ramp. The buildings were also simplified — a concrete Assembly House

A LAUNCHING RAMP CAMOUFLAGED INTO THE LAY-OUT OF A FRENCH VILLAGE.

NUMBER OF LAUNCHING SITES BUILT POINTING AT THE GREAT

PAS DE CALAIS.

FRANCE.

ASSEMBLY HOUSE CAMOUFLAGED AS A FRENCH BARN.

FIRING HOUSE CAMOUFLAGED AS A FRENCH COTTAGE.

CONCRETE PLATFORM.

FINAL ADJUSTMENT BUILDING MADE TO LOOK LIKE AN ORDINARY HOUSE.

FLYING BOMB IN LAUNCHING POSITION.

LAUNCHING RAMP CAMOUFLAGED AT SIDE OF ROAD.

THE FLYING BOMB, LAUNCHED BY CATAPULT OR OTHER DEVICE, ON REACHING THE REQUIRED HEIGHT FOLLOWS A DIRECT COURSE, BEING CONTROLLED BY ITS GYROSCOPE. WINDAGE, HOWEVER, MAY DEFLECT IT FROM ITS TRUE COURSE.

ATELY 7 DEGREES AND IS ABOUT 200 FT. IN LENGTH

GROUND LEVEL.

to which the flying bombs were brought in sections, a final adjustment building, parallel to the ramp to which the bombs were taken for setting of the gyroscope and a firing house with window slits of thick glass from which the launching was controlled. On leaving the ramp, the flying bomb soared to a predetermined height, levelled off on a straight course and headed for southern England — and the 18-by-20-miles target area presented by Greater London. On the way it met RAF fighters over the Channel, anti-aircraft gunners along the coast, more fighters over the Weald of Kent and finally the goalkeepers — barrage balloons protecting the approaches to the capital.

the body of the bomb; the outer track kept the wings trimmed. The whole device had great simplicity and it was part of the devilish incongruity of the entire invention that it should so exactly have resembled something which in peace time had given thousands of people thrills of screaming delight in every fun-fair from Coney Island to Blackpool.

The French people were, of course, well aware of the existence and location of these sites. It was possible to keep them hidden, or at least partly hidden, from the air, but not possible to keep them hidden from the farmers and peasants on whose land they were built. The new pre-fabricated sites could be transported and built in a few weeks. The much larger and more intricate sites from which launching power and supply came took as much as two years to build. On these the Germans built elaborate concrete storehouses with walls several feet thick, powerful block-houses, and large subterranean pumps for water supply. In many cases water had to be piped to the site from several miles away; railway tracks over similar distances had to be laid down to bring supplies; electric light and power had to be brought; intricate systems of concrete roads had to be laid in and about the villages and woodlands. All this had to be camouflaged with that thoroughness which is typical of the German nature. Every building and section of road was netted artificially or screened with boughs of such trees as pine, oak and fir.

The equipment of a flying bomb site consisted of nine major units:-

(1) The ramp itself is made up of eight six-metre sections containing a metal cylinder supported in a framework of girders, the cylinder having a gap 14.8mm wide all along its length. This gap is rather wider at the bottom of the ramp to facilitate the entry of the piston.

(2) A dumb-bell shaped piston fitting inside the ramp cylinder, and having a channel through each end parallel to the long axis, and carrying a lug to project through the gap in the cylinder, and so drive the bomb up the ramp.

(3) A small bore sealing pipe within the cylinder, of equal length, and held up tightly against the cylinder gap by lashings of wire every three metres.

(4) A cradle-shaped carrier block, known as the "Schlitton" (Sledge), on which the tail of the bomb rests during its transport to and passage

The bomb was brought to the base of the firing ramp where it was fuelled. It was then pushed onto the catapult and bolted down. In the background further missiles stand ready on trailers.

up the ramp.

(5) A "double deck" metal trolley for bringing up the bombs, known as the "Zubringerwagen".

(6) A rocket starter trolley providing the means to expel the piston and so launch the bomb, this trolley being known as the "Dampferzeuger".

(7) A fixed structure at the side of the ramp called the "Anlassgeraet", serving as a complicated distributor panel for the various compressed air and electrical circuits.

(8) The "Kommandostand" or firing pillbox from which the firing switches are operated.

(9) The bomb itself.

When the bomb had been successfully set in the Richthaus, it was brought to the base of the firing ramp, where it was fuelled, if fuelling had not already been done, and transferred to the ramp. The sledge was secured by means of an eye bolt and a six mm diameter steel pin to a split eye bolt on a bracket mounted at the base of the ramp. The rocket starter trolley was then brought into position and secured to the launching tube by a part turn of the bayonet fastening.

As soon as the circuit had been satisfactorily tested the connections were made to the bomb and the starter trolley and, two minutes before starting, the pressure reducing valve on the bomb itself was unscrewed. At this point all personnel retired to a safe distance and subsequent operations were carried out from within the firing pillbox. At the appointed firing time, the power unit switch in the pillbox was pushed over to the fully forward position marked "Teillast" (Part Power) and at the same time the switch marked "Start" was pressed. As a result of the first operation, compressed air was released via the Anlassgeraet to open the fuel feed valve to the power unit of the bomb and this air subsequently passed up into the combustion chamber. At the same time ignition occurred.

As a result of the second operation, compressed air was released in the cylinders of the rocket starter trolley and the combustion of the two propellants commenced. The bomb unit switch was held in the fully forward position for about three seconds and released so that it could spring back into the "Vollast" (Full Power) or intermediate position. The power unit then proceeded to run on full power for about seven

The rapid advance of the Allied armies in France was a great blow to the men at the launching ramps. The photograph on the left shows an unfinished projection site on the Cherbourg Peninsula, stormed by US troops in the last week of June, 1944. On August 23rd, Paris was liberated and the British and Canadian armies swept on towards Pas de Calais. Photograph in the centre shows the launching rails of a site not quite finished. In the foreground is the small control building. Below is the abandoned and damaged runway at Belloy-sur-Somme. The Germans retreated further to the east into Holland, re-directed their flying bombs and began to pound the great Belgian port of Antwerp.

seconds, the bomb being held stationary on the base of the ramp during this period until sufficient pressure had been built up behind the piston to cause sheering of the six mm retaining belt securing the rear of the sledge to the bracket on the ramp. When this happened the bomb shot forward and left the ramp at 400 kph.

When the bomb had been successfully launched, the sledge and piston flew through the air for a distance of 200 - 300 yards. Each site carried a number of both sledges and pistons and they were normally recovered at the end of the period of operation. After launching, the base of the firing ramp had to be hosed down by the members of the Einstelltrupp clad in rubber protective clothing. The preparation time required for the first launch of the day was at least 1 hours, subsequent launchings going more quickly. The record number of launchings at Houppeville was eight within a period of 14 hours.

Every site was in turn well protected by batteries of light and heavy anti-aircraft guns. The Germans, in fact, took every precaution to protect the V1 sites from the thing they feared most: the air. What they could not protect them from were two things and just as simple and elemental; the tongues of the French peasant and the animosity of the French towards their invaders. This is unfortunately not the place to tell the story of the Allied Intelligence services and what the people of France did for them; but it may be assumed that what French workers and peasants saw in the woods and villages of Normandy, Picardy and the Pas de Calais was ultimately what was seen by the bomb-aimers of the RAF and USAAF in the spring of 1944. It was also ultimately what was seen by thousands of British and Canadian soldiers as they rolled up the broken roads of the coast hinterland in the mad days of August.

But what the soldiers saw had a difference. What they saw could not be recognised as anything. What they saw again and again was simply a great ring of chalk— white bomb craters converging across the French fields to the nearest woodland, getting closer and closer until finally they actually touched each other, until the woodland and whatever had been in it was a meaningless and ghastly mess of concrete blasted into boulders and dust and of trees ripped to black and leafless skeletons. Behind the stilted words of scores of communiqués — "targets in Northern France and the Pas de Calais area" — lay a

American soldiers in Pas de Calais. The countryside is bleak with tragedy but liberation is close and the inhabitants of a nearby village are desperate for news.

violent piece of history.

Those launching sites were everywhere quite small and compact, quite the most difficult sort of target to find and quite well protected. Yet, in fact, practically every one of them had been discovered and blasted to pieces. It had not been uncommon for a launching site, in areas probably not much longer than a forty acre field, to receive on or about it as many as 4,000 bombs.

These incessant and successful attacks, in which both the RAF and USAAF suffered much loss, undoubtedly kept the scale of the flying bomb attacks down. The Germans rebuilt their sites again and again. They are even said to have offered increased pay to launching technicians, and as much as 1500 francs a day (about £7) to French workers who would assist at launchings but, whether these are mere fragments of French local legend or not, they seem to show the faith the Germans had in the weapon and their anxiety to keep up the rate of launchings in the face of attack from the air.

The fact that, throughout the winter, spring and early summer of 1944, the population of Northern France and especially the Pas de Calais, lived through hell is no legend. The countryside of the launching site is bleak with tragedy. Its villages have crumbled into heaps of stone and plaster; its fields are like miniature alpine ranges, unploughable until an army of bulldozers can level the countless bomb craters; village streets are chains of ponds after heavy rain; gardens and orchards have been obliterated. For the night and day bombing which caused all this the French had a single and terribly expressive word — *effrayant!* Yet again and again the observer talking to them in the days immediately after their liberation heard them say and could hear it only with deep emotion. "We did not mind, we were never afraid. However often you came and however much you bombed us we were never really afraid. We knew that it had to be done and that it had to be done to us. We knew that there was no other way."

The tragic and touching truth of these words was relieved, nevertheless, by some comedy. Again and again the French were delighted that the doodlebug, like a mad dog, turned on its masters. It showed a fairly frequent tendency to fly straight up into the air and fall on the crew; to fall short immediately after launching; to gyrate madly round and round and drop dangerously near those who had set it on its

During the winter, spring and early summer of 1944, the people of Pas de Calais lived through hell as RAF bombers pounded at the launching sites and suspected storage depots. Here a Halifax is over the target area where bursting bombs are sending clouds of smoke and dust into the air.

crazy course. The doodlebug, in fact, had failings that were almost human and the high rate of launching failures which the Germans had experienced at Peenemunde had certainly not been completely wiped out in France. And the French were delighted at this, not only because of a natural satisfaction in German failure, but because they knew that each one was a bomb less on England. Yet almost every one of those failures meant added distress and destruction to their own countryside.

Yet the man who visited the villages of the launching sites and came away with the impression that he had seen practically all that bombing could do would be very much mistaken. If he wishes to see something really gigantic in that way he should take the road south from the flying bomb country, through Amiens and southward on the Paris road, past miles of wrecked German transport and occasional buried German dead and sometimes a forlorn coal-burning German tank left by the roadside. He should go down the Paris road until he comes to the town of Creil, where the bridge across the lovely River Oise lies with its broken back in the stream. At Creil he should turn right, following the valley of the Oise and what was once a railway track, driving as best he can over what was once a road. He should go along this road, in comparison with which the blasted heath in Macbeth would be as pleasant as a seaside esplanade, until he comes to the village, or what is left of the village, of St Leu.

The valley of the Oise is broad and flat for a mile or two across and then is enclosed by steep low hills on either side. Down the valley the road, the river and the railway run, or once ran, parallel to each other. In the steep escarpment on either side lie the great underground stone caves of vast extent, from which stone has been quarried for building throughout centuries. On the south side these caves in peace time grew mushrooms for the Paris markets; on the north they still produced large quantities of stone, not unlike Cotswold stone, which gave to St Leu, Précy-sur-Oise and their neighbouring hamlets something of the appearance of the stone villages of England.

To the Germans these caves were a godsend. Too deep underground to be reached by bombs; of such area inside that they could hold almost unlimited quantities of material; easily reached by road, rail and river; they offered the perfect storage place for any weapon of war that had to be stored in safety and secrecy. In the caves of St Leu, therefore, the

Bombing attacks of storage depots had been carried out ever since a construction site, hidden in a forest between Calais and St Omer, had been spotted a year earlier. This was later shown to be a bomb-proof rocket launch pad in the Forêt d'Eperlecques which was so badly smashed by the US Eighth Air Force that the construction work had to be abandoned. Instead, the Germans built a factory to manufacture liquid oxygen needed to fuel the rockets and chose a replacement rocket bunker site in a quarry at Wizernes, ten miles away. This was repeatedly attacked but very little damage was caused until the RAF introduced the Tallboy — a Barnes Wallis 12,000 pounder with offset fins which spun as it penetrated the ground and then erupted like an earthquake. 617 Squadron dropped 32 Tallboys on Wizernes in June and July, 1944 and Hitler ordered that the site be abandoned. The picture below shows damage to a large concrete dome which covered the vast underground workings. See also page 157

Germans found the perfect home for their flying bomb supply.

They proceeded to adapt these caves with the greatest efficiency. They built branch-tracks up from the main railway to the cave entrances and even into the caves themselves, fitting them with unloading ramps and gantries. They floored the caves, throughout their ten kilometres breadth and depth, with concrete. They built inside them canteens, sleeping and living quarters, storage compartments for bombs. Outside, at the natural entrances, they shored up fissures in the rock with vast structures of reinforced concrete and walls of stone. They piped in water supplies and wired in electric light supplies. They deployed along the escarpment heavy and powerful batteries of guns. They worked in fact for two years on a great and clever scheme of adaptation.

On this work they had to employ a great deal of enforced French labour. Consequently it became an easy thing for the French to introduce selected members of the underground movement into labour gangs that did the work. The information picked up by these workers was filtered through, by processes which it is no part of this story to describe, to London. How accurate it was may be judged by the man who makes the journey along the road from Creil to St Leu and on to Précy; for that road, the railway running beside it, the branch tracks, the concrete by-ways, the block-houses, the gantries and everything else had, by September 1944, been blown to hell. All that remained, for miles and miles, was something like a huge river bed of mud and rocks from which a torrent had swept practically everything else away.

Among all the many names that the British people should remember in this war St Leu is by no means the least and they have good cause to remember it. For it was into the caves at St Leu that the Germans sent as many as thirty four train loads of flying bombs in a single day. Earlier, when the RAF attacked and blew up a train load of bombs, it was estimated that the train carried 200 bombs. The caves at St Leu therefore received in one day about 7,000 flying bombs for storage, or very nearly the same number as fell on Southern England in the three months of the summer. This was, nevertheless, only a tiny part of the caves' capacity.

In St Leu, therefore, the British people can see two important things; the extent of the German plan and power to destroy them and the extent

This was the first ground photograph of the RAF damage to the German flying bomb storage depot in the caves at St Leu d'Esserent. Thousands of bombs were dropped in a raid on July 5th, 1944, sealing one of the main entrances which led to a vast complex of galleries. In this raid the railway track at St Leu was cut in 20 places. See page 153.

of the French resolution to help prevent it. Through French help, bombers of the RAF and the USAAF helped to lessen greatly the strength of the attacks on England. They destroyed railways, trains and roads, they plugged up the entrances to the caves and in doing so they brought on the French people a degree of suffering of which the British people can never be too aware. The once beautiful valley of the Oise at St Leu is a valley of desolation. Yet the price paid for it by the French, which was part of the price of liberation, did not seem to them too great. "We were never afraid", was still their watchword. "And we know that if it was bad for us it was worse for you." In these words the French pay their own tribute to much that is best in their national character. For their intelligence, their courage, their faith and tenacity are as much part of the story of the doodlebug as the things that happened in England.

Another captured flying bomb site, this time at Fontaine-sous-Preax. Photograph shows jet propulsion unit discovered near a storage blockhouse.

This is the train load of 120 flying bombs, en route to the modified launching ramps, which was destroyed by RAF Typhoons in September, 1944. The train, in transit at the time, was blown to smithereens and the wreckage littered across a half mile square. All the Germans on the train were killed.

Photograph on the left shows a close up of the wrecked trucks.

By the beginning of August, 1944, thousands of gunners were assembled along the coast of south Kent and east Sussex. This most impressive shooting gallery included light and heavy anti-aircraft guns, American 88s, British 3.7s, a line of Bofors on high ground and rocket guns in the valley. Thanks to consistent practice and new radar equipment, the percentage of "kills" kept on rising — to 60 per cent by August 23 and then on to 74 per cent. On one night the total actually reached 84 per cent. Photograph shows Major General Cameron and Lt Col Land of Anti-Aircraft Command, in a 90 mm gun emplacement, congratulating American GI s for their accurate shooting. The picture was taken at Romney Marsh on August 18th, 1944.

CHAPTER NINE

The common shout of triumph

BACK in England, by the beginning of August things were reaching a new point of tension. By the end of July 5,258 flying bombs had been launched. They had caused 3,707 incidents overland, 1,807 incidents in London. About a quarter of them — 1,429 in fact — had been shot down by the RAF; 604 by AA fire; 158 by balloons; and 15 by HM ships operating in the Channel. Something like two-fifths of the bombs launched had been destroyed.

These relative figures are interesting. If we go back to June and July, before the large re-deployment by the AA guns over the English coast and take at random a day's activity, we shall see something like this.

Bombs Operating 125	Overland 77	London 48	RAF Destroyed 28	AA Destroyed 4	Balloons Destroyed 0	HM Ships Destroyed 0

The day is June 30th. The guns have not yet been re-deployed. They are still operating in the original plan already described. Their new equipment has not yet arrived from America. And the results are obvious. For every bomb destroyed by guns, the fighters of the RAF destroy seven.

Now take a day in August. And the figures become:

65	41	24	1	14	3	0

The day is August 1st. And now for every bomb destroyed by fighters the AA destroys 14. This is not necessarily a fixed situation typical of any day. On August 2-3, London's heaviest day, when in the 24 hour period 97 bombs fell, the figures are two for fighters and twenty five for guns. The conclusion is not, however, that the killing power of fighters was falling off, since the early days of August were obviously bad for fighter machines, but that the new AA deployment was an immense success. When the fighters can operate fully, as on August 31st, the figures become 23 for fighters and 29 for guns; and on August 4th, 31 for fighters and 32 for guns. On such days the killing power of fighters and guns is roughly equal and between them they destroy about half the bombs, on some days four fifths of the bombs, sent over in twenty four hours.

The change in the above situation over Kent and Sussex was in fact very great. Whereas in June and July the days had been full of a mad pandemonium of gun fire and fighters and flying bombs, with every villager wondering which among them was his greatest enemy, by August the new zones of operation were separate and clear. Whereas in the early days AA guns were destroying nearly one sixth of targets offered to them, by early August they were destroying about one half. The roar of coastal batteries, deep, powerful and practically continuous, could not only be heard but shook the windows of houses more than twenty five miles inland. The sound of the approaching doodlebug could be heard for about this distance too. The combination of these two sounds was electrifying. The explosions of doodlebugs being destroyed within the explosions of the guns was more electrifying still. Only when the guns ceased and there was either complete silence or the low level roar of an escaping bomb flying inland could a listener tell exactly what had happened.

These bombs had escaped fighters operating out to sea; the bombs escaping the guns were taken up by fighters operating inland. The stutter of machine guns in the country summer silence was just as electrifying as the sound of the guns. And the silence after the stutter of the fighter guns— that sure and terrible sign that the bomb had been shot down and was about to fall — was the most electrifying thing of all. For the people of Kent and Sussex it was the most exciting and unnerving thing of the war. It had in it all the drama but not the glory of the Battle of Britain.

The job of the fighter pilots was not easy. It is said that, before trying the campaign against us, Hitler had been confidently assured that no British fighter could overtake the flying bomb; and if it could we had no suitable ammunition to shoot it down. These assertions were proved ridiculous but the bomb was, nevertheless, a tough and difficult problem. It called for the last ounce of performance. It called for the employment of the highest speed Day Fighters, notably the Tempest, the Mustang, and the Spitfire XIV. Even so, aircraft had to be specially modified to give them enough extra speed to catch the bombs. Engines

Hitler was confident that no British fighter could overtake the V1. He was wrong. The Tempest V which could reach speeds of 416 mph at low level, was capable of consistently intercepting and overtaking the missile and the Tempest squadrons quickly found themselves in the front line of "Diver" missions. The three squadrons which formed 150 Wing, flying from Newchurch on Romney Marsh, led the battle in the air against the doodlebug. Flying up to 50 sorties a day, the Newchurch Wing claimed their 500th V1 in mid-July and their controllers threw a party in their honour. By August 23, their tally had risen to an incredible 623.

The new Spitfire XIV (centre) fitted with the powerful Griffon engine, was also a successful doodlebug destroyer and 91 Squadron and 322 Squadron were intensely involved in the anti-diver operations from West Malling in Kent. From here flew the Mustangs (bottom) of 316 (City of Warsaw) Squadron. The Polish pilots had another name for the doodlebugs — flying witches — for they seemed to cackle and laugh as they flew overhead. The Poles had the last laugh. By the end of July, 316 Squadron had claimed 50 destroyed.

were modified to accept higher boost and specially high grade fuel. Fighters were specially cleaned up and streamlined; mirrors and protruding gun barrels were either moved or fitted with streamlined covers. In this way as much as 30mph was gained in extra speed.

The chief difficulty, for the pilot, was to see the bomb. It was extremely hard to pick up visually by day at a range which allowed successful tactical approach. By night, because of its glowing tail jet, it could be seen from a long way off but the human eye was insufficiently sensitive to range. Sir Thomas Merton, however, produced a brilliant little range-finder at a cost of about one shilling which was a godsend. A special night Tempest squadron was formed, with very experienced night-fighter pilots and with great success. Its squadron Commander accounted personally for over 60 bombs.

Thirty four pilots in fact shot down more than ten bombs apiece. Two Tempest squadrons No. 3 and No. 486 shot down an incredible 580. No. 91 Squadron flying the Spitfire XIV, 96 Squadron with the Mosquito and No. 501 with the Tempest shot down over 100 each. Eight squadrons, among them Tempests, Mosquitoes, Spitfires and Mustangs, each shot down more than 50 bombs.

One of the fighter problems was to get enough warning of the bomb's approach. It meant that the attacks had to be dealt with mainly by standing patrols. During times of intense activity, 30 or 40 aircraft would be in the air continuously, night and day. In such long and exacting vigil the fighter pilot, lacking the exhilaration of combat with a human enemy, became tired, strained and often very bored. In spite of all this he had to keep very alert. The normal method of destroying the bomb was to approach to within 300 yards of it if possible and then shoot. The shooting had to be very accurate. If the pilot approached closer than this he was in danger of being blown up or, at the very least, damaged and put out of control. There were in fact very few casualties from this cause or from collisions in bad visibility or from flying into the ground in cloud from almost ground level: all of which is the greatest tribute to the skill and endurance and devoted airmanship of the fighter force.

There were two other methods of destroying a bomb by fighter aircraft. One was to fly alongside it and with very great skill and daring tip its wing so that it lost its balance and turned and destroyed itself.

Wing Commander Roland Beamont who commanded the 150 Newchurch Wing was Britain's first well-known fly-bomb ace, destroying 30 between June 16 and August 30. Beamont was also responsible for the tactics to be used against the V1. He recommended to Fighter Command that only the Tempest, Spitfire XIV and boosted Mustang be involved in Diver defences. He also had the guns on his Tempest altered to increase the effect of the firepower.

Squadron Leader Joe Berry who commanded the Night Fighting 501 Squadron at Manston set the record for V1's shot down in one night when, on July 23/24, he claimed seven. He enjoyed the challenge against the night intruders so much that he went on to destroy a record 61. 501 Squadron had many other Diver aces, including Flight Lieutenants Williams, Robb and Thornton, Squadron Leaders Parker and Rees and Flying Officers Deleuze and Miller.

Australian Flying Officer Kenneth Collier of 91 Squadron was the first pilot to fly alongside a flying bomb and tip it over with his wing tip so that it crashed. On July 23, 1944, he spotted a doodlebug that had been damaged by a fighter, but he was out of ammunition. Collier manoeuvred his machine up to the missile and used his wing "like a spoon" to throw the robot off course. It crashed near Tonbridge. This technique quickly became accepted and soon many airmen were employing the same method.

The first Polish fighter squadron to join the battle was 316, commanded by Squadron Leader Bohdan Arct. One of their heroes was Warrant Officer Tadeusz Szymanski whose daring exploit in chasing a doodlebug is featured on the front cover.

Wing Commander Leonard Cheshire, commanding 617 Squadron led the serious attack on flying bomb sites in December 1943. In later sorties, his courageous low-level marking techniques made pin-point attacks possible He went on to win the Victoria Cross.

Flight Lieutenant J.C. Musgrave had the distinction of being the first pilot to shoot down a V1. Musgrave, flying a Mosquito, with Flight Sergeant F. Somwell as Observer, of 605 Squadron encountered his "pilotless plane" in the early hours of June 16, 1944.

117

A fairly considerable number of bombs were so destroyed, some of them on occasions which saved the lives of people below. The other method, less common but still more daring, was to fly in front of the bomb, throwing it out of control by the fighter's slipstream. These were unorthodox and emergency methods used when the pilot had run out of ammunition. By all methods the RAF destroyed, by its fighters alone, nearly 2,000 bombs in eighty days.

There is a significant piece of RAF/Army co-operation work which must not be forgotten here: searchlights. We have seen how very difficult it is for the human eye, insensitive to range, to judge the distance and speed of a flying bomb at night. In the first nights of attack, before modifications had made night fighters faster, the Mosquito was hardly fast enough to catch the bomb. It needed the added speed of a dive to enable it to intercept. Its attack was, therefore, a turn towards the bomb at about a mile above it, then a flat-out dive with the pilot turning as he pulled out level and finally a period of steadying a level course before the aircraft lost the impetus of the dive and the target pulled away. It was the searchlights who told the pilot, during that dive in the dark, exactly where his target was. With the aircraft travelling at six or seven miles a minute they needed to work with the greatest accuracy. A dive held for a few seconds too long meant a death-crash for the pilot. A straying searchlight would dazzle the pilot and crew, with the same result. Yet out of 466 pursuits, in which night fighters and searchlights co-operated, not one fighter was lost in this way.

The searchlights had other difficulties. For the new low target, light had to be re-sited, to give a better view. They had to be swung faster and lower yet with more accuracy than ever before. If the number of kills in which they helped was rather small — about 140 bombs — that number was, nevertheless, 30% of the total bombs flying by night into the searchlight area. To all this they added the valuable work of giving roof-spotters in London an early warning of approaching bombs. And through all of their work, which called for great speed and skill and accuracy and patience, they helped to save many lives.

The game of the doodlebug was the fastest ever played on a small field. The task of co-ordinating all weapons — fighter, searchlight, guns, radar, balloons — in so small an area and in so short a time, was

To attack a flying bomb at night, the
fighter pilot would fly about a mile
above it and then power-dive
through the darkness with the pilot
turning as he dived to pull out level
with and a little behind the bomb.
Finally there was a short period of
steadying down and adjusting the
range to shoot before the impetus of
the power-dive had worn off.
Squadron Leader Joe Berry, the
greatest doodlebug night fighter of
all, knew this manoeuvre would not
have been possible without the
searchlights which indicated the
course of his quarry. On the ground
it was a task that called for skilled
and accurate operation for the
slightest error could have resulted in
the pilot being dazzled, with
disastrous effects. The searchlight
batteries contributed enormously to
the destruction of 30 per cent of all
doodlebugs which entered this
illuminated arena.

ATS girls operating searchlights

immense. The performance by radar, and of that all too often un-sung organisation the Royal Observer Corps, was at all times magnificent. This splendid voluntary organisation, without whose tireless work the Battle of Britain could not have been fought and won, had long claimed the proud distinction of being able to plot and name every kind of aircraft that flew, whether by night or day, seen or unseen, alone or in numbers. To this the doodlebug proved no exception. From its isolated posts on hills and lonely sheep-marshes, church-spires and seashores, fields and harbours, the ROC plotted the doodlebugs in thousands and had as its reward the dangerous privilege of seeing and hearing the greater part of them shot down above and about them. No-one can praise the men and women of the ROC enough for their steady twenty-four-hour-a-day work in this most dismal of all air battles. The whole Raid Reporting System of which they were part was utterly essential for the successful defence of the country. In two ROC centres RAF controllers were installed, to work the fighters from there. The first flying bomb to appear over the country was immediately recognised as such and was instantly reported, so that within a few seconds the whole defence organisation had been informed.But not only was the information supplied by the Raid Reporting System used for the immediate defence of the country. By careful computation and analysis it provided information on which Bomber Forces could attack landing-sites across the Channel. The ROC also fired special warning rockets, known as snow-flakes, that gave to pilots a rough indication of the route of flying bombs. ROC posts on the fringe of the balloon barrage also fired red warning rockets to turn aside the early pursuing fighters.

The erection of so large a barrage as now strung itself out on the chalk slopes or among the great beech woods by the North Downs, had never before been attempted. The swiftness of its assembly, by which balloons were rushed southward from the northern, western and midland cities they had so long protected, was so great that it dazed even the men themselves. And the result dazzled all of us who saw it. To come up from the south country by train, through the long tunnel in the Downs, and emerge into the clear blue of early summer day and see overhead hundreds and hundreds of sailing white balloons, serene and glistening above the light ground mist of the hills, was the only pleasant experience the doodlebug ever gave.

These two Observers spotted the first flying bomb to cross the coast. Mr A.M.Wraight (with the binoculars) and Mr E.E.Woodland were on duty on the night of June 12th-13th at Post Mike Two, a Martello Tower at Dymchurch, Kent when they spotted a robot making a noise "like a Model T Ford going up a hill". Mr Woodland seized the telephone and made a Diver warning to Maidstone ROC centre (right). The plotter at the group centre reacted immediately. "Diver, diver, diver", he called across the room. The sirens sounded and the message was relayed to Fighter Command. The flying bomb flew on to Swanscombe in Kent where it crashed harmlessly in a field.

But behind this loveliness lay very realistic things. No one knew at first how the doodlebug would behave when it hit the cables. The first one arrived at night, exploding as it struck the cable. This was quite unexpected, and other bombs did the same, giving none of the information desired; namely how far the bomb would travel after it had struck the cable. This information was essential in view of the fact that between the barrage and London there were many populated areas in which it would be costly for bombs to fall. A day or two later there arrived, at about 2,000 feet, the first of many bombs to hit the cable and go on. The effect was rather like that of a fish taking the bait from a gigantic hook below a gigantic float. The fish wriggled forward in a series of sideward darts, wagging its tail for a distance of about 400 yards, and then gave up.

This was excellent, though it was not necessarily all that was wanted. It was clear that the balloon cables would stop bombs; but it was clear also that more balloons were needed. The number of balloon squadrons was, therefore, at once increased and extra cables were hung from all balloons. The engineers of the GPO, of whose magnificent work in wiring gun-sites, balloon-sites and Observer Corps sites and repairing bomb-damaged telephone cables everywhere, all too little has been heard, provided phenomenal extensions of telephone wiring to hundreds of new sites in a short time. Kills soon began to increase and with the increase in kills an increase in all organisation, since every bomb brought down by a balloon meant a new balloon, enough pure hydrogen to inflate it and the re-wiring of its cables. Sometimes these cables were scattered about the countryside, and had to be retrieved. All this vastly increased the work of operators and the pressure on supplies.

From 17th June to 31st August the following supplies were used by one squadron of balloons alone:-

Hydrogen	*18,830,800 cu. ft*
Main Cable	*142 miles*
Light Cable	*57 miles*
Transport Mileage, including	
hydrogen delivery to site	*121,403 miles*

But this vast expenditure of material was very well worthwhile, when it is seen that one squadron alone destroyed 37 bombs.

The scene at a balloon site where a flying bomb was brought down by a cable and crashed onto farm buildings at Tatsfield, Surrey.

WAAF balloon operators learn how to handle a balloon before manning a site and relieving the men for other duties.

Splendid though the work of balloons was, and with it the work of fighters, searchlights and Observer Corps, it was really the guns that found, in August, the most magnificent revival of form. Their early work against the bomb had undoubtedly been disappointing. That "wild and inaccurate" shooting, so early noted by the army's own official observers, had not been lost on the people of the countryside. In the same way the splendid revival by August was clear to them also. No one could fail to miss the dramatic fury of their new success. In the first seven days after that huge deployment in July, the coastal batteries shot down 17% of their target. In a week it was 40%, and in the fifth week it had more than trebled itself to 55%.

These figures, wonderful though they are, can give no idea of the dramatic clamour of a great gun-barrage firing above the sand and shingle and white cliffs of the southern coast with a solid roar. There had been nothing like it before in England. It was, indeed, not uncommon during these roaring August days, to hear 30 or 40 bombs shot down in one of the saturation attacks which the Nazis so favoured; or to see as many as ten bombs shot down simultaneously, simply disintegrating into the air in brief bursts of fantastic flame. Remember too that all this was blind shooting: the dream of the robot defence against the robot attack. The eyes that found the range and the target were robot eyes; the loading and prediction and firing were automatic. Through this Wellsian combination of mechanical ingenuities, backed by human sweat and blood, the percentage of kills rose by August 23rd to 60%; and in the last week of the battle to 74%. More expressive even than this, the guns during one night reached the figure of 82%, and in one magnificent day in August shot down 68 out of 96 bombs, of which only four reached London. This also is the place to note that of all the heavy batteries operating along the Southern coast, one eighth were American. Much of the very latest equipment was also American and of the bombs shot down by fighters, a few were shot down with immense sporting zest by Americans, though they were not, officially, assigned that delightful task.

It would not be right, either, to allow the superb performance of the guns to cancel an equally superb performance, carried on for a much longer time, by the bomber forces of the RAF and the American Air Force under General Spaatz. They pounded the launching-sites in France and Germany for a whole year. They dropped on these targets

The Royal Navy also played its part in the battle. This is Tonsil, an experimental anti-flying bomb battery. It was a rush job; the projectors were mounted on rockets in two days and the complete battery of 10 projectors was ready for action between Hythe and Dymchurch within four days of the order being given on July 15th. On July 20th, Tonsil scored its first kill and by the end of the month it had shot down eight flying bombs. In August, the battery was enlarged to 20 projectors capable of firing 400 rockets at once.

GIs on Romney Marsh, Kent helped to combat the doodlebugs. Here are the men of B Battery, 125th American Anti-Aircraft inside their director (predictor) dugout.

100,000 tons of bombs and in doing so, they lost 450 aircraft, among them many heavy and medium bombers, and nearly 3,000 men. To these men we owe tribute and gratitude for which there is no material shape. Hideous and wretched though life was in Southern England through the days of the late summer, it would have been infinitely more dangerous if it had not been for these men. British and Americans together shared the job of delaying and lessening the enemy attack. By giving their lives, by giving them literally in thousands, they saved the lives of others, possibly in tens of thousands.

If it had not been for their combined efforts the attack would in fact have begun in January. It would have been launched at the time of the year when there was little daylight, when fighters and balloons were often grounded, when AA crews would have found conditions discouraging and hard. New equipment would not have been available. The bombardment would have begun much earlier, would have been much heavier and would have gone on much longer.

Remember, therefore, above all the percentages and figures and tables of comparative official data, the courage of these men. It was a courage that had most of its publicity in a tedious and necessary repetitive communiqué — "military installations in Northern France and the Pas de Calais area". For every person killed by a flying bomb at least two others are alive because of a year of operations by these men. Men of whom 2,900 did not live to see the fruit of their splendidly human endeavour against the newest of science's barbarities towards their fellow men.

From Italy the Prime Minister, as the fly bomb attacks from French launching sites came to an end, sent a telegram of congratulation to the gunners:

"Many congratulations on the brilliant work of the anti-aircraft batteries which has more than borne out what we did hope for them."

That telegram, sent to one Command, will in fact serve for all commands who gave everything they had, men and women, time and energy, sweat and death, to beating the menace that was to have wiped London off the map, made life in Southern England insupportable, and ultimately to have made the invasion of Europe a failure. The quietness that came down on the harvest fields and full orchards and rich hills of the South in early September had in it, for all those who cared to hear, the common shout of triumph and gratitude for all that had been done and for those who had lost their lives in seeing that it was done.

Girls in a mixed Ack-Ack battery march smartly to their operational duties. This is not the life they expected to live but there was a job to be done and they were relieving the men for other duties.

The Air Ministry in a report published in November 1944 acknowledged that the results of the V1 offensive were "greatly in the enemy's favour". It cost the Allies nearly £48 million in aircraft and airmen lost, bombs dropped, shells fired and balloons lost, and that did not include the many millions of pounds spent repairing and rebuilding homes in southern England.

The production cost of each V1 was approximately £150 and the Germans spent in excess of £12 million on constructing launching sites and training the crews.

Had the flying bomb attacks on England come a few months earlier, it is possible that the war might have taken a different course. As it was the attacks followed the Normandy landings and, thanks to the men and women of all commands, the menace that was to have wiped London off the map was a failure.

Since the bombing of Peenemunde in August, 1943, the rocket programme seemed to have been abandoned, but this was far from the case. Rocket trials had been moved to Blizna, 170 miles south of Warsaw and out of reach of the British bombers. Peenemunde had been rebuilt and experiments with missiles resumed and the assembly of rocket components had been moved to Dora, a gigantic underground factory, near Nordhausen in the Harz mountains of Central Germany.

Sandys' speech to a crowded press conference on September 7th, in which he said that the Battle of London was over, could not have been more ill-timed, for the Germans were actually preparing to launch their first V2, a weapon that was designed to annihilate the civilian population of London.

The Nazis had intended the launch to be from huge concrete firing bunkers, but this was abandoned after heavy bombing by Flying Fortresses. Instead they introduced a Meillerwagen — a mobile firing table. The rocket battery moved to The Hague in Holland and prepared for a double launch against London.

CHAPTER TEN

A warning for the future

BY the end of the first week in September the Allied armies had swept so far beyond the Normandy battlefields and so far up the North French coast and its hinterland of drives and woods and villages and so far beyond the beginning of the Flanders plain that the chances of flying bomb attack against England from land bases seemed to be over. When Mr Duncan Sandys, MP made a long statement to the press on September 7th, giving this very assurance together with the compressed details of the campaign, the attack had lasted 80 days. There was, in fact, still a second attack to come.

Before the final ejection of the enemy from the northern areas of France there had been a period when some flying bombs seemed to be launched from bases farther east. It seemed possible that these came from sites in Holland. They tended to fall north rather than south of the Thames, notably in the riverside part of Essex and the Northern boroughs of the metropolis. There was nothing to distinguish them from bombs launched from the coast of France.

From Wednesday September 6th to Friday September 15th, no flying bombs fell on England at all. The only enemy activity against this country was the continued vicious shelling of Dover, Folkestone and the Kentish coast from long-range gun batteries in the not yet captured port of Calais. This shelling continued until Tuesday, September 26th, when 50 shells fell in the town of Dover in a single day, depriving half the town of its water supply and sending most of the population into shelters. As the Canadians closed in, this was the last demonstration from Calais' enormous guns. A day later three flying bombs fell in Essex; two days later two fell in the same county, one in Hertfordshire, one in Cambridgeshire and three in Suffolk. In these very rural and sparsely populated areas no one was hurt. Two days later still, three bombs fell in Essex, one in Cambridge, one in Hertfordshire, one in Kent and one in Sussex. Thereafter flying bombs continued to fall in a series of irregular attacks in roughly the same proportion on the same counties. These attacks never had the seriousness or weight of the attacks made in Kent and Sussex and

London in the summer and it was not until October that the City of London itself was hit again.

By this time the method behind all these easterly attacks was known. It was clear that they were made not from bases in Holland but from parent aircraft operating over the North Sea. This possibility had long been foreseen, and the method known as that of the pick-a-back plane, by which bombs were carried on parent aircraft, released and guided on to their target by means of radio controlled automatic pilot. This knowledge was inaccurate only in that it was later discovered that the bomb was carried not on the back of the aircraft but under the belly. The method of its launching remained the same. Fitted with a rocket propulsion unit instead of a jet propulsion unit and a fuse detonated by radio-impulse and not by impact, the HS293 version of this kangaroo-like weapon was about half the size of the land-launched bomb which had come in thousands over Kent and Sussex. Its weight was 1,760 lbs, its maximum speed in free flight about 300 mph. It could be carried under the wings of several German aircraft, notably the Dornier DO217E5, the Focke-Wulf FW200C.Condor, the Heinkel HE177A and Junkers JU290.

While these sporadic attacks from air-launched bombs were bringing to East Anglia something of the tension and pain that Kent and Sussex and London had known much more intensely during the summer, something else was happening. The shadow of its rumour had begun to creep about London as early as September. Occasional large explosions both by day and night had the inexplicable effect of giving a second report, like a vast echo, some seconds after the first. These noises remained officially unexplained, either from British or German sources, for two months after they had begun. During this time, though never critically frequent, they had occurred often enough to give the rumour a shape and a name. The shape, said gossip, was a drainpipe; the name was the long-threatened, long-expected and, it is only fair to say, long-apprehended V2.

It was not, in fact, until November 8th that the German High Command announced at the beginning of its daily communiqué that Revenge Weapon No 2 had been for some weeks in use against London and targets in Southern England. The timing of the announcement was interesting. It appeared to have been dictated by the special associations

Werner von Braun (right), a scientist with a passion for rocketry and space exploration and Captain Walter Dornberger, an artillery officer in the German army were the brains behind the V2 rocket, a technically brilliant but hated weapon which was both the ancestor and forerunner of all subsequent ballistic missiles. The two men are seen here at a dinner to celebrate their first successful launch on October 3rd, 1942. It was at this dinner that von Braun said: "Today space travel was born". The German army, the Wehrmacht, however, was always more interested in the military capabilities of the rocket and a devious power struggle developed within the Wehrmacht and the Nazi establishment. This had much to do with the creation of the rocket. Below, Nazi leaders watch a rocket trial. In the centre, shielding his eyes is Josef Goebbels, Propaganda Minister. Albert Speer, Minister of Munitions, is on the right.

which November 8th, the anniversary of the Munich Putsch, has always had for members of the Nazi Party. On this occasion the date was more interesting than usual. The formal anniversary celebration had been postponed and Hitler had neither a speech nor an appearance to make to his people. As a substitute for these momentous omissions the announcement that V2 had been intensively attacking London for some weeks was no doubt considered to have comforting importance to the German homeland. The official communiqué was followed by various propaganda talks, evidently held in cold storage in which "the gratitude of the Homeland", was expressed to "the workers who 'despite every turn' had made the achievement possible", and in which there was some tribute to the heroism of troops on launching sites, troops "who knew the sufferings of the Homeland under enemy terror from their personal experience." To these were added the usual acid gibes at the British Government for so unobligingly keeping quiet about the whole affair; some threats that V2 was only the first, or the second, of a complete series of trump cards; and some geographical information. "The London railway station of Euston was completely destroyed," the German listener was told, "and police have ruthlessly roped off this part of the town." In subsequent versions of the talk Euston became Epsom, near London, but whether the target had been salts or horseflesh the speaker did not say.

German propaganda was very clear on two things. It was quite sure of the vanity of the struggle of the British people against V2. It was equally sure, and was at pains to point out, that "V2 alone could never decide the war in favour of Germany," a point which had been put forward in consolation by so many British newspapers to their readers. "We," said German propaganda, "have never said it could. But we would only say that Germany, despite very heavy air raids and all the strains and burdens of the sixth year of war, has been able to produce another completely new weapon and to employ it effectively." Of other things German propagandists were not quite so sure. They were not sure, to within at least 100 miles, where the rockets were falling, and it is no part of this story, for obvious reasons, to enlighten them. Nor were they very sure of its appearance and effect, and on that point called in a number of those convenient Swiss and Swedish observers who from favourable neutral positions on the mountain passes of their

The V2 rocket was unreliable and there was never any certainty that it would lift off. Like the V1 it had a tendency to turn on its masters. Many were launched from built-up areas in Holland, such as The Hague where streets were blasted when the missile misbehaved. This picture was taken during an early trial.

countries are in some way able to observe and describe events at distances of up to a thousand miles. Some of these Swedish observers conveniently noted how "before the missile falls to the ground from the stratosphere with a roaring sound, a weaker explosion is audible, which is immediately followed by the actual impact, combined with a gigantic white flame. The velocity of the fall is immense owing to the enormous altitude and amounts, according to V2 estimates, to 1,600 km an hour."

On November 10th, Mr Churchill made a statement in the House of Commons: "Last February", he said, "I told Parliament that the Germans were preparing to attack this country by means of long-range rockets; and I referred again to the possibility of this form of attack in my statement in this House on 6th July.

"For the last few weeks the enemy has been using his new weapon, the long-range rocket, and a number have landed at widely scattered points in this country. In all, the casualties and damage have so far not been heavy, though I am sure the House would wish me to express our sympathy with the victims of this as of other attacks. No official statement about the attack has hitherto been issued. The reason for this silence was that any announcement might have given information useful to the enemy, and we were confirmed in this course by the fact that, until two days ago, the enemy had made no mention of this weapon in his communiqués.

"Last Wednesday an official announcement, followed by a number of highly coloured accounts of the attacks on this country, was issued by the German High Command. I do not propose to comment upon it except to say that the statements in this announcement are a good reflection of what the German Government would wish their people to believe, and of their desperate need to afford them some encouragement. I may however mention a few facts. The rocket contains approximately the same quantity of high explosive as the flying bomb. However, it is designed to penetrate rather deeper before exploding. This results in somewhat heavier damage in the immediate vicinity of the crater, but rather less extensive blast effect around. The rocket flies through the stratosphere, going up to 60 or 70 miles, and outstrips sound. Because of its high speed, no reliable or sufficient public warning can, in present circumstances, be given.

"There is, however, no need to exaggerate the danger. The scale and

Chairman of the Crossbow Committee, Mr Duncan Sandys told a crowded press conference on September 7 that, except possibly for a few last shots, the Battle of London was over. "The understanding of the people of Kent, Surrey and Sussex is deserving of great praise", he said. "By their readiness to accept their share of London's dangers, the people of bomb alley played a notable part in keeping down the overall casualties." He also had special praise for the Americans. "They have thrown themselves into the job of beating the bomb with just as much determination as if New York or Washington had been the victim of the attack." The two men on Sandys' right are General Frederick Pile and Sir Roderick Hill. In the background is Sandys' military adviser, Colonel Kenneth Post.

effects of the attack have not hitherto been significant. Some rockets have been fired at us from the island of Walcheren. This is now in our hands, and other areas from which rockets have, or can at present be fired against this country will, doubtless, be over-run by our Forces in due course. We cannot, however, be certain that the enemy will not be able to increase the range, either by reducing the weight of the war-head or by other methods. Nor, on the other hand, can we be certain that any new launching areas which he may establish further back will not, also in turn, be over-run by the advancing Allied Armies.

"The use of this weapon is another attempt by the enemy to attack the morale of our civil population in the vain hope that he may somehow by this means stave off the defeat which faces him in the field. Doubtless the enemy has hoped by his announcement to induce us to give him information which he has failed to get otherwise. I am sure that this House, the Press and the public will refuse to oblige him in this respect."

Mr Churchill's statement, giving no secrets away, nevertheless contained enough hints to show that here at last a phenomenal Wellsian dream had come true within the life of its creator. Its dimensions, its range, its speed and its entire robot behaviour seem, on examination, like part of an impossible fantasy. This streamlined projectile, 45ft 10ins long, 5ft 6ins in diameter, with its sharply pointed nose and four external fins at right angles to each other in its rear, flies at a maximum speed of about 5,000 feet per second. It is faster than sound. It rises to a height of 60 or 70 miles above the earth. It travels in a parabolic path to an average range of 170 miles, with a maximum so far observed of 220 miles. Theoretically it can do more than all this. It can attain velocity up to 6,800 feet per second, and a range of up to 340 miles. Since it flies faster than sound itself there is no warning of its approach. The sound of its approach follows the projectile itself to earth and is heard, like an echo, when the sound of its explosion has died away. This accounts for the double report that distinguishes the rocket wherever it falls from the flying bomb.

These sounds are vast and can be heard for distances of at least sixty miles. The warhead that causes the first of them weighs 2,150 lbs or just under one English ton. It is part of a total weight of 12.2 tons, of which 8.5 tons is fuel. It is detonated by a fuse which must give

The day after Duncan Sandys' press conference, a V2 rocket, weighing 13 tons and armed with a ton of high explosive hurtled towards London via the stratosphere at a speed of more than 3,000 miles an hour. The missile ended its brief but deadly flight at 6.43 pm on Friday September 8th, 1944 in the western suburb of Chiswick. The explosion in Staveley Road created a 30-foot wide crater; three were killed and 17 seriously injured. As it hit the ground the people of London heard a double thunderclap — the impact and the noise of the rocket breaking the sound barrier. This was the turning point in the history of warfare. Chiswick was the first place in England to be introduced to the long range ballistic missile.

instantaneous action, since the rocket approaches the ground with a speed of 2,500 feet per second. Its area of casualty effect is about 80 per cent larger than that of the flying bomb, though its area of damage is about the same. Its crater, in contrast to that of the flying bomb, is about 10 to 12 feet deep. Processes of velocity at great speed have sometimes caused the rocket to explode in the air: a problem that without doubt seems to have given German scientists a good deal of trouble. In some of the incidents so far recorded in England, the rocket has broken up in the air, its components disintegrating and falling to the ground, when the warhead has exploded in the normal manner. It is possibly because of these problems of overheating that V2 has not yet attained the theoretical range of 340 miles. It remains, nevertheless, an ingenious and diabolical robot conception translated into fact. It belongs to a world of hideous phenomena. It comes without sound, without warning and without discrimination. Its inaccuracies are so vast that it becomes a weapon of monstrous chance, neither aeronautic nor military in its value and power.

Defence against this projectile that precedes the sound of itself flying through space offers none of the opportunities of the doodlebug. Neither the modern fighter, though flying at more than half the speed of sound, nor the modern anti-aircraft gun, itself almost entirely robot in its behaviour, can usefully be brought against it. A stratospheric balloon barrage, trailing cables sixty miles long, would be as effective as a spider's web against its parabolic path. So far as science has announced anything approaching a theory of defence, any solution against it in flight seems to be a considerable way before us, in a future less and less marked by pleasantry in war. Meanwhile the obvious and only methods of attack against it are attacks on its launching sites and the simple but fundamental solution of occupying the country which launches it.

The second of these solutions being a matter of time, it remains only to consider the first. As with the launching sites of the flying bomb, the launching sites of V2 are small, well dispersed and well or ingeniously concealed. In concealing them the German High Command showed again their complete disregard of civilian property, and civilian casualty, this time Dutch instead of French, excelling themselves once more in their genius for selecting sites in streets,

The first two rockets to land in Britain were fired from Walcheren Island in Holland. Many more were launched before British Commando Troops with British and Canadian Infantry landed on the Island and smashed the coastal batteries barring the way to Antwerp (see picture). This forced the German batteries to withdraw to south-west Friesland where an ideal site was found in a thickly wooded area close to the hamlet of Rijs and well concealed from the prying cameras of Allied reconnaissance aircraft. The V2 had a 200-mile maximum range and the cities of Norwich and Ipswich were the only sizeable English centres now within firing range. Between September 26th and October 12th, 30 rockets landed in East Anglia and more than a dozen in Essex. All fell harmlessly and there were no fatalities. By November, Antwerp was in Allied hands and the rocket units were instructed to destroy it completely. More than 100 V2 rockets pounded the city killing hundreds of people — the worst attack coming in December when a missile landed on top of the Rex Cinema. It was packed at the time and 567 were killed of which 296 were Allied servicemen and women.

between rows of houses, or even between the buildings of hospitals. To attack such targets successfully is extremely difficult. To bomb them heavily, with large bombers, would have been disastrous to civilian life. The answer to the problem they offered lay in a new kind of precision bombing: a new kind, that is, for the aircraft that performed it.

It was on November 21st that the RAF announced that, for purposes of dealing with these small and difficult targets, the Spitfire had become a bomber. On that day it was told how bomber-Spitfires had made a successful attack on V2 storage, erection and launching installations in a Dutch wood, where a rocket was in fact waiting to be fired. Bombs on the installations and strikes of strafing on the rocket itself were the measure of the day's success. From that time onward Spitfires continued, often in appalling weather and throughout the daylight hours of the winter, their fast and precise attacks on similar targets. In a period of five days more than 25 separate attacks were made:all in the face of vicious anti-aircraft defences. Fighter patrols all over Holland also made many attacks on supply lines or rail and road leading to more of these Serdergerstadschutzplatz: by which grandiose and humourless name the German knows his rocket site.

Weeks of special training were necessary to fit these Spitfire-bomber pilots for their new precision tasks. When the German High Command built a rocket-store and firing installation within 300 yards of the historic Dutch royal palace, Huis ten Bosch, the House in the Wood, now a cultural museum at the Hague, it may not have been in the hope that attacking Allied bombers would hit the palace rather than the installation, and thus alienate Dutch friendship, but the thought is possible. Royal Australian Air Force squadrons, however, put all their bombs on the right target in a single attack, and other Spitfires attacked it later on. Similarly when the Germans installed V2 equipment in the grounds of an hotel, and ran a V2 railway siding into a narrow gulley between a housing estate and a hospital, it may not been with the object of securing for them a privileged kind of protection, but the thought is again possible in a book dealing, in its several ways, with monsters. Spitfires again, with fine accuracy, bombed the site, the trains and the rocket and left houses and hospitals unharmed. In power dives from 8,000 feet through cloud-gaps they demonstrated once again how flexible, adaptable and deadly air-power can be in the hands of those

The railways were very much part of the London battlefield. Twenty eight rockets scored direct hits on railway property and no fewer than 358 affected the railway network to some extent. Picture above shows the bridge over Southwark Park Road, Bermondsey which took a direct hit on November 5th, 1944 and collapsed into the roadway. Below is the damage at Angerstein Wharf on March 7th, 1945. The Southern Railway came off worst from the two V weapons — 63 were killed on railway property and 767 injured.

who understand its uses.

Do the Germans understand its uses? It may be correctly argued that the rocket-projectile has nothing to do with aeronautics or air-power. Basically it is a long-range shell. It differs only from the shell projected by long-range artillery in that it carries its propellant inside it, and is sometimes controlled by radio — sometimes by an integrating accelerator that cuts off its fuel when correct velocity has been attained, instead of being propelled from the barrel of a gun. It is in a sense the larger dream-version of the Big Bertha by which the Germans shelled Paris in World War I and which had negligible effect on the course of that war. But V2 is also a commentary on German understanding of air-power and for the simple reason that it does not form, in its present uses, a supplement to the ordinary bomber and its bombs, but is a substitute for them. Its final effect is that of a bomb weighing about a ton. In 1940 and 1941 the Germans understood elementary air power enough to drop such weight by means of aircraft piloted by men.

Today, (early 1945) as I write, the Luftwaffe stands somewhere aside on the bleak and shrinking frontiers of Germany and watches a fifth of that weight of explosive projected by super-intricate and laborious devices in which there is none of that touch of combatant glory they knew in the summer of 1940 above English fields. The stratospheric rocket that pounds to earth in the dark night of Southern England is not an advance, in any kind of way, on the bomb that once shattered the Cathedral of Coventry or the Guildhall in London. It has less accuracy, less point, less flexibility, less effect. In grimly insulting the German Air Force it also takes war one retrograde step nearer the robot world of Capek, one decade nearer the controlless lunacy of Frankenstein. Carried to that extreme, it makes a mockery of men who "in their thousand chariots to the battle fly".

The people of south-east England have suffered grievously from the V2. During a busy Saturday lunchtime a missile impacted itself to the rear of Woolworth in New Cross Road and the store collapsed in a great cloud of smoke and dust which mushroomed high up into the air. The store was full of women and children and the death toll was 160. It was the worst V weapon tragedy of all.

Though the attacks by it have always been more sporadic and widely spread than those of V1 they have been supplemented by the first

With the decision to stand down the Home Guard and with the Allies still pushing deep into occupied Europe, everyone thought the war would be over by Christmas, 1944. But as the festive season approached, it seemed more than ever like a bitter slog, particularly with such an effective German counter-offensive in the Ardennes. As another year dawned, rockets continued to pound London several times a day and the occasional air-launched doodlebug caused more tragedy. March was the crisis month for the Nazis but still there was unremitting fire from the rocket batteries in The Hague, including one that dived directly onto the centre of Smithfield Market (see picture) on Thursday March 8th at a time when the market was packed with traders and customers. It penetrated the floor, exploded into the underground network below and the buildings collapsed into the crater. 110 people were killed.

weapon, launched by parent aircraft, so that in fact parts of England have had to suffer a double trial. All that has been said in previous pages about firemen, defence workers, policemen, builders and defence organisations generally — and perhaps we should not forget here the trained dog that came into use in late autumn as a means of finding buried victims — is equally true of this second phase.

Winter is not kind to the bombed. It is a little better, but not much, to be bombed in summer. Snow and gales and much rain throughout the English winter of 1944-5 placed on victims and firemen and builders and defence workers a strain that seemed all the tougher after the trials of the summer. They were, as always, heroic. Fragments of their tenacity and suffering constantly seep in far behind the bleak frontage of the official secrecy of "some casualties were caused", and show them to have been as unconquerable as ever. The visitor to England who said: "There are parts of Southern England that remind me of Pompeii" was perhaps not a million miles from the truth. The effect of V1 and V2 alike are rather less pretty than those of the volcano. But morally he was wrong by stratospheric distances. Pompeii died and was obliterated. Southern England continues passionately to be a living emblem among her green fields and woods and dreaming spires.

Nevertheless, the figures, relating for the most part to the three distinct phases of the V1 campaign and the rocket attacks which followed (see pages 154 and 155) are part of the measure of her ordeal. The list is nothing more than the barest summary of the heroism and havoc, terror and wretchedness, organisation and expense that were the cost of the flying bomb. It gives no record at all of the humanity, the neighbourliness, the little decencies, the small self-sacrifices, the kindnesses and the untold millions of cups of tea that helped to make life tolerable in its time. No book on Britain could, however, be complete without some mention of the cup of tea, that national emblem and restorative through which we all survive. Enough to say that in Beckenham, much-bombed south-eastern suburb, receiving 69 bombs, 101,407 teas were served by the WVS alone in ten weeks, or a rough average of 2,000 cups of tea per bomb per day. In Woolwich the inhabitants who survived its 75 bombs drank from the mobile canteens alone 20 gallons per day. Even in Kensington, that popular London combination — the cup o'tea and buttered bun, had more than 53,000

Casualties have been taken to hospital after many hours' punishing work for the Civil Defence workers and rescue squads. Now it's time for a short break and the regulation cup o' tea from the WVS mobile canteen.

customers.

Figures, it has been said, begin by inspiring a man and end by putting him in a straight jacket. Figures may relate; they cannot restore. They may record; they cannot relieve. These figures are almost entirely figures of human loss, human suffering, material loss, material ugliness, the disaster of material power. They form a precious record of part of a single summer for which the British, the French and no less the American people have paid bitterly. Properly read, in clear perspective, they are a warning and a triumph. They are a triumph for that unanalysed and mysterious human process, sometimes known as the Life Force, against the forces that are constantly devised to destroy it but never do. They are a warning for the future of the undeclared war, the unheralded bomb, the pilotless plane, the robot stratosphere rocket, limitless in range and size. They are a triumph of human endeavour, human decency, human sacrifice and great human courage. They point forward to a future rocket of the limitless possibilities of the use of scientific power. They show only part of the price paid by humanity for civilisation and the kind of civilisation humanity gets in return: only the beginnings of what life may be like in great cities in future wars.

 **1945**

Time eventually ran out for Hitler and his troops. On March 24th, 1945 the Western Allies advanced across the Rhine and the rocket men had time for a few parting shots before moving out of Holland. The last V2 was fired on March 27th and landed in Orpington where Ivy Millichamp, a young housewife, was killed — the last British civilian to be killed by enemy action. As the rocket sites were vacated, advancing commandos came across many souvenirs. Mr G.D. McElwee, a trooper with the "Phantom Unit" supplied this picture of an abandoned train carrying a number of rockets. He found German civilians frantically filling up cans and containers with rocket fuel.

This photograph came from Mr White of Essex and shows "Bert on a doodlebug".

As the Allied advance continued, the vast underground rocket factory at Dora near Nordhausen in the Harz Mountains of central Germany was overrun by marines of the 1st US Army in April, 1945. Here they found one of history's greatest technical prizes — undisturbed assembly lines of flying bombs and rockets in 10 miles of interlaced tunnels. There were enough rocket parts to fill 300 large railway wagons, sufficient to construct 75 V2's. That was not all. The Americans discovered that Hitler's "miracle weapons" had been produced by prisoners in unimaginable conditions. Some 60,000 able-bodied POW's, of 21 nationalities, had been forced to work in the hell of Dora's tunnels and at least 20,000 of them died. While the Vengeance campaign was at its zenith, the death rate at Dora was simply too high for the camp's crematorium to cope. The ovens were hot when the Americans arrived but scattered around, as far as the eye could see, were as many as 6,000 unburned corpses. They were mainly middle-aged men, reduced to skeletons, who had simply been worked to death. Before they left, the Americans blew up the entrance to seal the complex.

Few of the people marked for "termination", such as Gipsies and Jews, were working in the factory. It was not intended to be a death camp and, in fact, was not even mentioned in the literature of the Holocaust. However, Dora was an SS camp and mass murder did take place. In 1947, just one administrator and 18 officers were tried for war crimes but the trial records were then classified by the US army. Historians believe that the Americans wanted to suppress the embarrassing truth that many German scientists were given contracts to pioneer the US space programme, including Werner von Braun, Arthur Rudolph, the civilian head of "V" production at Dora, and 500 members of the former Peenemunde team.

Flight Lieutenant Jack Stephens DFC, pilot 207 Squadron, Main Force.

Warrant Officer Jack Pegrum DFM, Wireless O/Gunner 207 Squadron, Main Force.

Squadron Leader "Pil" Pilgrim DFC, Pilot, 44 Squadron, Main Force.

Flight Lieutenant Geoffrey Whitten DFC, Navigator 35 Squadron, Pathfinder Force

Squadron Leader Norman Scrivener DSO DFC Navigator 83 Squadron Pathfinder Force.

Squadron Leader Charles Lofthouse OBE DFC Pilot 7 Squadron, Pathfinder Force.

Squadron Leader Anthony D.Lambert DFC, Pilot 620 Squadron, Main Force.

PEENEMUNDE VETERANS

On the moonlit night of August 17th, 1943, 596 bombers of 54 Squadrons set off across the North Sea in a bid to destroy the workshops and laboratories where the V2 rocket was being designed and manufactured. It was one of the biggest and most important raids of the war and one which claimed the lives of many airmen. More than fifty years later, seven members of the "Peenemunde club" were invited to RAF Hendon, the home of Bomber Command, to sign Frank Wootton's painting of that great raid. These survivors, who represent the hundreds of brave men who took part in "Operation Hydra", include members of both the Pathfinder Force and the Main Force.   (See page 37)

This photograph records the actual moment that Dr Werner von Braun (with a broken arm), Major General Walter Dornberger and Herbert Axter, a senior scientist (hatless) surrendered to troops of the 44th Division of the US Army. They were arrested in a village close to the Bavarian town of Oberammergau where they had stored large quantities of drawings and documents.

In the autumn of 1945, von Braun and his rocket team settled in America to help with a new V2 programme. Six months later, the first American rocket was launched from a "new Peenemunde" — the White Sands testing ground in New Mexico — from where von Braun referred to himself and his colleagues as "prisoners of peace".

All restrictions on the German scientists were lifted and by 1955 von Braun was an American citizen and in charge of the Apollo Space Project. His greatest dream eventually came true. On July 20th, 1969, he heard these historic words from astronaut, Commander Neil Armstrong: "Houston. Tranquillity Base here. The Eagle has landed".

Throughout his scientific life, von Braun had maintained that his object in developing the V2 was for space exploration and not weapon development and, on one occasion, he was even arrested for refusing to work exclusively for the SS. The fact remains that the rocket was the

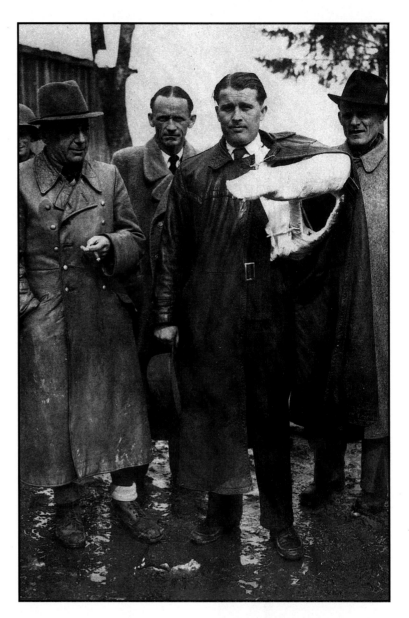

most effective weapon designed and one with which Hitler could well have won the war had it arrived a little earlier.

It was January, 1944 before the first V2's rolled off the production line but they never reached the levels demanded by The Führer because von Braun and his scientists insisted on a constant stream of modifications to the design, some 63,000 changes in all.

It was a masterpiece of scientific and engineering brilliance but it cast a shadow that still hangs over the world today.

The V2 rocket, so feared by those living in southern England, soon became a museum piece. This one was erected in Trafalgar Square after the war and, in subsequent years, they were placed in the Imperial War Museum and the Science Museum. In October 1945, two captured rockets were test - fired from Cuxhaven in northern Germany for the benefit of the Allied Air Defence Division under 'Operation Backfire'. They came close to their intended target in the North Sea. In Britain, France and Holland, they live today in the memory of people who were either bereaved by the bombs, or bore the scars of terrible injury. These include the fighter and bomber pilots who lost more than 2,900 colleagues in the V Weapon campaign.

More than 50 years after they were discovered and bombed, the remains of flying bomb 'ski sites' are very much in evidence in various parts of Pas de Calais. Photograph above, taken in January 1994, shows the launching ramp, aligned on London, at Bois Carré, just a few miles from Abbeville. Thanks to the resistance network, led by Michel Hollard and the Mosquito pilots of photographic reconnaissance, the Bois Carré site was the first to be identified. The broad-arched entrance (below) gave the clue that whatever weapon was being prepared here had wings — possibly Hitler's pilotless plane. The scars remain from the bombing in October 1943.

The entrance to the limestone caves at St Leu d'Esserent, just north of Paris where flying bombs were stored. The caves, containing an extensive system of underground galleries, were repeatedly bombed, one of the biggest raids coming on July 4th-5th, 1944. A section of the caves is used today for a small industrial concern, but, as a result of the raids, the great galleries remain sealed. See also P. 109.

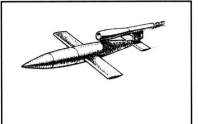

Between June 13, 1944 and March 29, 1945, a total of 9,251 flying bombs were plotted. Of these, 2,419 evaded fighters, gunners and balloons to crash in London. The total number destroyed was 4,261 — 1,971 by anti-aircraft guns, 1,979 by the Royal Air Force, 278 by balloons and 33 by the Royal Navy.

The Doodlebugs

A total of 2,419 fell in the London Civil Defence Region during the main attack from June 13 to September 1, 1944. Croydon received the most with 141. Here are the figures for each borough.

Croydon 141	**Carshalton** 27	**Barnes** 9
Wandsworth 122	**Twickenham** 27	**Hampstead** 8
Lewisham 114	**Bexley** 25	**Richmond** 8
Camberwell 80	**Leyton** 24	**Kingston** 8
Woolwich 77	**Wanstead** 23	**Chingford** 8
Greenwich 73	**Malden** 21	**Acton** 7
Lambeth 71	**Surbiton** 20	**Staines** 7
Beckenham 70	**Kensington** 20	**Shoreditch** 7
Orpington 63	**Chigwell** 20	**Southall** 7
West Ham 58	**Enfield** 20	**S Newington** 7
Coulsdon 54	**St Pancras** 19	**Edmonton** 7
Chislehurst 45	**Walthamstow** 17	**Cheshunt** 6
Mitcham 43	**Penge** 17	**East Barnet** 6
Poplar 39	**City of London** 17	**Hayes** 6
Barking 37	**Fulham** 15	**Finchley** 6
Bromley 37	**Hornsey** 15	**Southgate** 6
Beddington 36	**Heston** 15	**Wood Green** 5
East Ham 36	**Islington** 15	**Finsbury** 5
Hackney 36	**Willesden** 15	**Uxbridge** 5
Esher 35	**Wembley** 14	**Paddington** 5
Merton 35	**Hammersmith** 14	**Feltham** 5
Banstead 35	**Southwark** 14	**Barnet UDC** 4
Battersea 34	**Hendon** 13	**Ruislip** 4
Sutton 34	**Brentford** 13	**Sunbury** 4
Ilford 34	**St Marylebone** 12	**Holborn** 4
Wimbledon 33	**Erith** 12	**Tottenham** 4
Bermondsey 30	**Crayford** 11	**Yiewsley** 3
Deptford 30	**Harrow** 11	**Chelsea** 3
Stepney 30	**Ealing** 11	**Elstree** 2
Epsom 29	**Waltham**	**Bushey** 1
Westminster 29	**Holy Cross** 11	**Frn Barnet** 1
Dagenham 28	**Bethnal Green** 9	**Potters Bar** 1

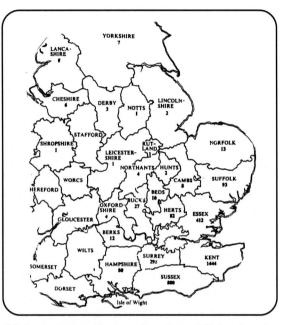

Of the counties, Kent endured most flying bombs with 1,444 crashing on land and a further 1,000 shot down in the sea. Altogether 448 communities in the county reported damage and some suffered time and again. During the first week of the campaign, 101 were shot down in Kent and the incidents after that occurred on average, at the rate of 20 a day. Deaths from the doodlebugs in Kent totalled 156 with 1,716 injured.

The map shows how the bombs were scattered far and wide over the other counties, including 880 in Sussex, 412 in Essex and 295 in Surrey.

The communities in Kent and East Sussex to receive the most flying bombs were as follows: Tenterden 238, Ashford 184, New Romney 149, Sevenoaks Rural 137, Malling Rural 97, Tonbridge Rural 95 In East Sussex: Battle Rural 374, Hailsham Rural 159, Uckfield Rural 146.

Between September 8, 1944 and March 27, 1945, 1,115 V2 rockets were fired at Britain, killing 2,612 people in London and 212 elsewhere. London received 517 and 537 fell outside the capital. The V2 took just five minutes from launch to impact and travelled too high and too fast to be tracked down.

A total of 537 rockets fell in eleven English counties with Essex bearing the brunt of the attack, with 378. Kent, 64 and Norfolk, 29 were the next highest and many, of course, fell in the sea. The maximum height attained by the missile was estimated at 328,000 feet and the maximum speed 3,500 mph. Hundreds more rockets were destined to land on British soil but the Allied armies gained the initiative and the rocket pads were overrun.

307,672 mothers and children left the London area under the official evacuation scheme. 4,615 expectant mothers left London. 38,341 aged people left London. 12,550 blind people left London. 500 special trains were run. 10,000 houses were seriously damaged. 107,000 houses were totally destroyed. 700,000 houses needed repairs.

The Rockets

A total of 517 V2's fell in the London Civil Defence Region as it was in September 1944. Ilford was the recipient of most rockets with Woolwich a close second. The full list of boroughs and missiles received is:

Ilford 35	**Hackney** 10	**Tottenham** 3
Woolwich 33	**Deptford** 9	**Southwark** 3
West Ham 27	**Poplar** 9	**Finsbury** 3
Greenwich 22	**Camberwell** 9	**Lambeth** 3
Barking 21	**Edmonton** 9	**Hampstead** 3
Dagenham 19	**Enfield** 9	**Banstead** 2
Walthamstow 18	**Islington** 8	**Elstree** 2
Chislehurst 17	**Stepney** 8	**Battersea** 2
Erith 17	**Bermondsey** 7	**Bethnal Green** 2
Waltham	**Cheshunt** 7	**Shoreditch** 2
Holy Cross 15	**Bromley** 6	**S Newington** 2
East Ham 14	**Wandsworth** 6	**St. Pancras** 2
Wanstead 14	**Crayford** 5	**Westminster** 2
Orpington 14	**Beckenham** 5	**Heston** 2
Chigwell 13	**Willesden** 4	**Wood Green** 2
Bexley 12	**Harrow** 4	**Ruislip** 2
Lewisham 12	**Hornsey** 4	**Hayes** 2
Leyton 12	**Croydon** 4	**Hendon** 2
Chingford 11	**Southgate** 4	**Richmond** 2

One rocket fell in each of the following boroughs: **Staines, Holborn, Potters Bar, Barnes, East Barnet, Barnet Urban, Yiewsley, Ealing, Wembley, Finchley, Friern Barnet, Sunbury, Twickenham, Brentford, Hammersmith, Kensington, Chelsea, St Marylebone, Esher, Kingston, Coulsdon.**

No rockets fell in the following: **Bushey, Uxbridge, Southall, Feltham, Fulham, Acton, Paddington, City of London, Malden, Wimbledon, Surbiton, Merton, Mitcham, Penge, Epsom, Sutton, Carshalton, Beddington.**

This painting by Frank Wootton records the moment on August 4th, 1944 when Flying Officer Dixie Dean of 616 Squadron "elbowed" a doodlebug out of the sky. Dean, who was flying the twin-engine Gloster Meteor — the RAF's first high-performance jet fighter — dived on his prey at 450 mph but, when his cannons failed, he flew alongside and performed the "Polish circus trick".

The blackest day for Kent in terms of fatalities came at dawn on Saturday June 24th when a V1, shot down by a fighter, crashed onto the Newlands Military Camp at Charing. The 47 men who died were buried at Lenham. These wrought iron gates which lead to the cemetery stand as a memorial to that tragedy. The incident occurred less than a mile from the Bates' home in Little Chart.

The impressive remains of the gigantic factory, launch pad and bunker in the Forêt d'Eperlecques between Calais and St Omer, which was abandoned after US bombing in August, 1943. Below: The replacement bunker and rocket storage facility at Wizernes. The massive cupola, five metres thick, shows the scars of Tallboy. See page 107. The photographs were taken in January, 1994.

ACKNOWLEDGEMENTS AND CREDITS

THE cost of the Vengeance Weapon campaign was enormous — 8,958 dead and 24,504 injured — a total that could have been much higher if the V3 had ever been put to use. This was housed in a great concrete structure at Mimoyecques, near Calais which contained 50 smooth-bore barrels, approximately six inches in diameter and 416 feet long. It was planned to fire finned projectiles, each weighing about 300 lbs, at a combined rate of up to ten a minute at London. Despite production difficulties, the development of this scheme was being pursued enthusiastically in Germany but the construction was heavily bombed and never came into action.

Prof. R.V.Jones in his book *The Secret War* explained that the V3 was called Hoch Druck-Pumpe (High Pressure Pump) and when news of its purpose reached London there was a feeling that British Intelligence, so successful against the V1 and the V2, had failed. He is certain, however, that had the V3 approached a degree of success in trials comparable with that of the other V weapons, they would probably have heard more about it.

I am grateful to Prof. Jones and all the other military historians whose books I have referred to for information that was not available to H.E.Bates. These include Norman Longmate's *The Doodlebugs* and *Hitler's Rockets*, Constance Babington Smith's *Evidence in Camera*, General Frederick Pile's *Ack-Ack*, Charles Graves' *Women in Green*, Pratt Boorman's *Kent Unconquered*, After the Battle's *The Peenemunde Rocket Centre* and *The Blitz (Volume Three)*. I have also referred to a variety of pamphlets, newspaper articles, documents and official files from the Public Records Office. Considerable help has come from the Curator of Dover Museum, Mr John Iveson, Mrs Diane Searby, widow of Group Captain John Searby, Mr Tony Smith of the Hastings Exhibition Centre, Mrs B.M.Plunkett and many members of the public.

I would also like to mention my own book *Doodlebugs and Rockets*, which is available in paperback and hardback and follows the story of the vengeance weapons from concept to conclusion, using many maps, diagrams and statistics. There are numerous letters and anecdotes. It was during my research for this book that I came across the Bates manuscript.

Bob Ogley 1994

THE PHOTOGRAPHS

Photographs provided by courtesy of: Helena Szymanska-Cullum 2. Madge Bates 7, 146. The Trustees of the Imperial War Museum, London 12, 15 (top), 17, 36, 38, 43, 45, 47 (bottom), 48, 54, 57, 63 (top & bottom) 69, 79, 81, 83, 85, 89 (top), 90, 101, 105, 107 (top & bottom) 109, 110, 111, 115, 117 (middle top & bottom), 119(bottom), 123, 125 (top), 135, 143, 145. Punch 18. Evening Standard 13, 53. Mrs Mavis Hurley 15. Topham 20, 103, 139, 151. Bundesarchiv, Koblenz 22, 128, 131 (bottom). Deutsches Museum, Munchen 32, 33, 128, 131 (top), 133. The Illustrated London News Picture Library 24/25, 96/97. Kent Messenger 27, 51, 60, 119 (top & bottom), 91, 121 (top), 127. Constance Babington Smith 31. Croydon Advertiser 87. Kentish Mercury (Lewisham Local Studies) 77. National Railway Museum 141 (bottom). London Fire Brigade 141 (top). Fern Flynn 35, 117 (top left), 152 (top & bottom), 153, 156 (bottom), 157, 160. Diane Searby 37. John Haybittle 41. Mavis Hurley 15 (bottom). Croydon Libraries Department 59, 65, 71 (bottom) 75, 100 (top). Mrs Bohdan Arct 117 (bottom left). P.R. Earl 55. Local Studies Library, London Borough of Newham 71 (top). Mr G.D. McElwee 147. Mr White 147. Mrs L.M.Gay 148. Holly Pelling 149. Frank Wootton 156.

Doodlebugs and Rockets,
by Bob Ogley is published
by Froglets Publications
£16.95 (hardback)
ISBN 1 872337 22 8 and
at £9.95 (paperback)
ISBN 1 872337 21 X

We would like to thank the Bates family for their great help and support.

INDEX

The royalties of this book are being given to the RAF Benevolent Fund by Madge Bates, pictured here in 1994 in front of the ruins of the old church at Little Chart. It was here she stopped to take a picture when walking with H.E. on one of their first visits to the area in 1930.
She recalled some of the happier memories connected with this church. It was in the adjacent fields that son Richard went strawberry picking, giving H.E. the inspiration for the famous scene in The Darling Buds of May.